Buildbox 2.x Game Development

Build rich, high production value mobile games and distribute them across different platforms with Buildbox

Ty Audronis

BIRMINGHAM - MUMBAI

Buildbox 2.x Game Development

Copyright © 2016 Packt Publishing

First published: September 2016

Production reference: 1260916

Published by Packt Publishing Ltd.
Livery Place
35 Livery Street
Birmingham
B3 2PB, UK.
ISBN 978-1-78646-030-1

www.packtpub.com

Credits

Author

Ty Audronis

Reviewer

Nik Rudenko

Commissioning Editor

Ashwin Nair

Acquisition Editor

Reshma Raman

Content Development Editor

Sachin Karnani

Technical Editor

Rupali R. Shrawane

Copy Editor

Safis Editing

Project Coordinator

Ritika Manoj

Proofreader

Safis Editing

Indexer

Mariammal Chettiyar

Graphics

Abhinash Sahu
Jason Monteiro

Production Coordinator

Nilesh Mohite

Disclaimer

The projects and raw files included with this book are free to use for learning purposes. However, be advised that if you attempt to distribute a carbon copy of Ramblin' Rover (even if by another name) to any distribution channel, that channel may cancel your account. This decision lies solely with the channel, neither the Author nor Packt Publishing has a say in it. Duplications, such as this, are forbidden by the EULA (End User License Agreement) you agreed to, with your distribution networks.

Foreword

At Buildbox, we're extremely passionate about the creation of games. It is our livelihood, and we believe games themselves to be the ultimate in artistic expression. Video games combine core elements from every major art form. They fuse animations, pictures, technology, and sound into an immersive experience like none other. When you view a painting or watch a movie, you can see a beautiful world on display, but when you play a game, you are *inside* that beautiful world. You are the hero of that world and you are 100% responsible for their journey. You, as the protagonist, must hone your skills of the game to decide their fate. This immersion causes a very close connection to the games people play; a connection that is much stronger and more emotionally attached than most forms of art. Proof in point—there are many more people with tattoos of The Legend of Zelda than the Mona Lisa. They are both great pieces of art, and the Mona Lisa is arguably more famous, but The Legend of Zelda has definitely affected more people on an emotional level.

If there is one hobby more fun than playing games, it's *creating* them. Making the game, testing, tweaking, and finally watching it go live is something only a few will experience, but they will all tell you it's amazing. This especially rings true if you see strangers playing your game on the subway, or when you watch the facial reactions of your friends playing your game for the first time. There is something truly special about creating joy for others, and games do this in a very special way. When you make games, you are doing more than just creating code. You are creating experiences for other people.

Unfortunately, the problem with creating games is inherent in their design. To create something that is an accumulation of all art is not an easy task, and before Buildbox, options were very limited. In fact, with an estimated 17 million programmers on Planet Earth, only 0.2% of the population could create a game. Our goal with Buildbox was to help the other 99.8% of the people who might be interested. It was a difficult task, but we've been very excited to cultivate a new style of software—and an amazing community—over the past 2 years. This journey hit a major milestone a few months ago with the release of Buildbox 2.0. This new version expanded the software in a large way by adding in over 150 new features. Some of these were major additions such as multiple worlds, multiple characters, and an expanded menu system with animations. Other features were more under the hood, but still required to make vastly expanded gameplay.

It's been a very exciting ride so far, and when Packt Publishing reached out about creating this book, we were excited for two very important reasons. First, we are not only fans of Packt, but also customers. Things have come full circle as the development team here at Buildbox has purchased multiple Packt books in the past to help create various aspects of the software. Second, we understand that while tools are great, you are only as good as your training. With Buildbox, there are many best practices, undiscovered tips, and hidden secrets that can vastly improve your game making experience. Inside these pages, you'll find all of those and more. The author, Ty Audronis, has an amazing insight into the software regardless of how complex the issue is at hand. Also, our CTO, Nik Rudenko, was the technical editor. Nik single handedly coded the first version of Buildbox and has been instrumental in its success. No human on the planet knows Buildbox better than him.

Finally, there has absolutely never been a better time than right now to make a video game. As of 2015, more people are spending money on video games than movies, music, or TV. The market has matured, the app store is proven, and mobile has won the race. Everywhere you turn people are glued to their phones, looking for the next app to download. What will they download? Will it be your game? There is no reason it shouldn't be. In the last 18 months, more than 75 Buildbox games have been featured by Apple or broken the Top 100 of the app store. These are games made by regular people—the 99.8% of us that don't know how to code. With this book and Buildbox, you'll have all the tools you need to do it yourself. Time to get started.

Trey Smith

Founder of Buildbox

About the Author

Ty Audronis has been creating games and interactive experiences on computers since 1980. When other children were earning money for trips to convenience stores and arcades by raking leaves or mowing lawns, Ty was helping neighbors buy computers, and programming games for the neighborhood kids on an Atari 800 computer.

In the 1990s, Ty was introduced to the Internet and was attending California State University, Chico, as a visual effects major. He had an epiphany; one day there will be no difference between film, television, games, and the Internet. Everything will converge. As a result, Ty diversified his education (and career) into all things media. Luckily for Ty, he was right.

He's worked on several apps and games for various clients using several different development platforms. Ty has worked in many great institutions (from Frog Design to California Academy of Sciences and beyond). Ty has been recognized in several industries for his artistic and technical exploits and abilities. These include studio design, workflow design, post-production for TV/film, marketing, digital design and development, and even as a drone pilot and builder.

Ty has authored two other books for Packt Publishing: *Lightning Fast Animation with Element 3D* and *Building Multicopter Video Drones*.

I'd like to personally thank all those who have helped in the creation of this book. From my partner in crime and editor, Sachin Karnani, to the gracious and personable CEO of Buildbox, Trey Smith, and CTO, Nik Rudenko, without whom this book would not be nearly as informative as it stands. I'd also like to thank the users of Buildbox on the forums, who have been instrumental with their help, especially these users: yenomeerf, telerebor, heathclose, and Andy (the Admin). Also, I cannot forget the Buildbox support team. Their patience and diligence in supporting their product is certainly commendable and outstanding. To my family, friends, and mentors: thank you to my father, Tony Audronis, for introducing me to technology at a very early age. To my wife for reading through this book with me chapter-by-chapter and correcting my many typos and errors. For standing by me through the years and all the struggles we've endured. To my children who gave up a majority of their summer vacation daddy-time with no complaints while I wrote this book. And to my mentors: thank you, and I hope this book (and my career in general) have made you proud.

About the Reviewer

Nik Rudenko has more than 15 years of game development experience. He originally started his career as a 3D artist, but quickly found himself being drawn to the technical aspect of making games. After earning degrees in both graphical design and computer programming, Nik merged his knowledge of graphic concepts and coding to master the art of game development.

While he was working on AAA games such as Overlord, Pirates of The Caribbean, and Show Time Boxing, he always had the dream of one day building his own game engine. Nik wanted to create an engine that could help art designers that didn't know how to code, make games.

After multiple successful game projects for iPhone and Android, he moved to America from the Ukraine where he started working on his dream project—Buildbox.

I would like to thank my father, who was a Ukrainian teacher. He instilled the important values of education, hard work, sacrifice, and family. He saw my passion for computers and used all of his savings to buy a modern PC for me, and that very first CD disk with 3D Graphics Software was a major turning point in my life.

www.PacktPub.com

For support files and downloads related to your book, please visit www.PacktPub.com.

Did you know that Packt offers eBook versions of every book published, with PDF and ePub files available? You can upgrade to the eBook version at www.PacktPub.com and as a print book customer, you are entitled to a discount on the eBook copy. Get in touch with us at service@packtpub.com for more details.

At www.PacktPub.com, you can also read a collection of free technical articles, sign up for a range of free newsletters and receive exclusive discounts and offers on Packt books and eBooks.

https://www.packtpub.com/mapt

Get the most in-demand software skills with Mapt. Mapt gives you full access to all Packt books and video courses, as well as industry-leading tools to help you plan your personal development and advance your career.

Why subscribe?

- Fully searchable across every book published by Packt
- Copy and paste, print, and bookmark content
- On demand and accessible via a web browser

Table of Contents

Preface

This book is designed for two purposes.

First, to give you the necessary familiarity with the Buildbox interface, as well as the process of getting your games distributed to players.

Second, to be a reference guide in the future if you find yourself stuck. We tackle many of the most common issues that developers face when using Buildbox.

We use a tutorial method to follow the entire game building process within Buildbox, by leading you through the full process of game development; from design, to development, to distribution, you will gain the necessary knowledge to create your own games. We even cover monetization strategies so that you can make your games profitable!

Whether you're a beginner or an experienced programmer, you'll find this book helpful while discovering that Buildbox is a great tool for quick-turnaround game creation for mobile and computer games.

What this book covers

Chapter 1, *So, You Want to Develop a Video Game?*, is designed to set the expectations of the reader, and get them excited about the journey that they are about to embark on.

Chapter 2, *Orientation*, is an orientation to the game development environment within Buildbox by touring a template of a basic game.

Chapter 3, *Your First Game – Ramblin' Rover, Part 1*, will cover setting up the game's structure and create the first world of our motocross-style game.

Chapter 4, *Advanced World Design – Ramblin' Rover, Part 2*, will cover adding advanced controls and obstacles to our first world.

Chapter 5, *Menus, UIs, Sound, and More! – Ramblin' Rover, Part 3*, will add the finishing touches to our game by adding menus, user interfaces, and audio.

Chapter 6, *Monetization – Ramblin' Rover, Part 4*, will walk through how to set up advertising accounts, and set up your game for in-app advertising. We will also talk about monetization models using coin shops, video rewards, and more!

Chapter 7, *Exporting your Game and Compiling for Various Platforms – Ramblin' Rover, Finale,* is followed by the summary of this chapter.

Chapter 8, *Building Other Popular Game Types,* covers some tips and tricks for making other popular game types with Buildbox.

Chapter 9, *Buildbox Tips and Tricks,* is a quick reference of procedures for certain tasks and reference a for some settings within Buildbox.

What you need for this book

You'll need a Mac or PC that meets the minimum specifications for Buildbox. You should also have either a trial or full license for Buildbox version 2.x. Having graphics software such as Gimp or Adobe Photoshop is highly encouraged, but not required (as for the examples in this book we have created the assets for you). Similarly, having some sort of audio editing software (such as Adobe Audition) is highly encouraged, but not necessary.

Who this book is for

This book caters to those who have an interest in or desire to create their own mobile games as a hobbyist, or who are looking to enhance their skills as a professional games developer. No coding experience is required.

Conventions

In this book, you will find a number of text styles that distinguish between different kinds of information. Here are some examples of these styles and an explanation of their meaning.

Code words in text, database table names, folder names, filenames, file extensions, pathnames, dummy URLs, user input, and Twitter handles are shown as follows: "Mount the downloaded `WebStorm-10*.dmg` disk image file as another disk in your system."

New terms and **important words** are shown in bold. Words that you see on the screen, for example, in menus or dialog boxes, appear in the text like this: "The shortcuts in this book are based on the Mac OS X 10.5+ scheme."

 Warnings or important notes appear in a box like this.

 Tips and tricks appear like this.

Reader feedback

Feedback from our readers is always welcome. Let us know what you think about this book-what you liked or disliked. Reader feedback is important for us as it helps us develop titles that you will really get the most out of. To send us general feedback, simply e-mail feedback@packtpub.com, and mention the book's title in the subject of your message. If there is a topic that you have expertise in and you are interested in either writing or contributing to a book, see our author guide at www.packtpub.com/authors.

Customer support

Now that you are the proud owner of a Packt book, we have a number of things to help you to get the most from your purchase.

Downloading the color images of this book

We also provide you with a PDF file that has color images of the screenshots/diagrams used in this book. The color images will help you better understand the changes in the output. You can download this file from http://www.packtpub.com/sites/default/files/downloads/Buildbox2xGameDevelopment _ColorImages.pdf.

Errata

Although we have taken every care to ensure the accuracy of our content, mistakes do happen. If you find a mistake in one of our books-maybe a mistake in the text or the code-we would be grateful if you could report this to us. By doing so, you can save other readers from frustration and help us improve subsequent versions of this book. If you find any errata, please report them by visiting http://www.packtpub.com/submit-errata, selecting your book, clicking on the **Errata Submission Form** link, and entering the details of your errata. Once your errata are verified, your submission will be accepted and the errata will be uploaded to our website or added to any list of existing errata under the Errata section of that title.

To view the previously submitted errata, go to https://www.packtpub.com/books/content/support and enter the name of the book in the search field. The required information will appear under the **Errata** section.

Piracy

Piracy of copyrighted material on the Internet is an ongoing problem across all media. At Packt, we take the protection of our copyright and licenses very seriously. If you come across any illegal copies of our works in any form on the Internet, please provide us with the location address or website name immediately so that we can pursue a remedy.

Please contact us at copyright@packtpub.com with a link to the suspected pirated material.

We appreciate your help in protecting our authors and our ability to bring you valuable content.

Questions

If you have a problem with any aspect of this book, you can contact us at questions@packtpub.com, and we will do our best to address the problem.

1
So, You Want to Develop a Video Game?

Games are fun, and they're super cool. They've quickly replaced baseball as America's favorite pastime (heck, the world's for that matter). But with teams of hundreds of people developing games for major development companies, how do indie developers, small companies, or even marketing agencies keep up with the amount of work to get a game to market in time? Enter Buildbox, a code-free game development tool for mobile and desktops alike.

What Buildbox can (and can't) do

Before we really get started, let's set some expectations. Just like a contractor building a house, a video game developer has several tools in their toolbox, each with their own purpose. Although these may (at times) overlap, each development platform has its strengths and weaknesses.

Buildbox is a truly code-free solution for developing video games. You won't be developing any **First Person Shooter** (**FPS**, such as *Call of Duty*) games using Buildbox, nor any (**Massive Multiplayer Online Role Playing Games** (**MMORPGs**, such as *World of Warcraft*). But what you can do is quickly develop entertaining mobile and computer games that are 2D or 2.5D (isometric).

And that's why you should choose Buildbox to develop such a game… speed. In fact, what you'll find through the course of this book is that the most time-consuming part of using Buildbox isn't actually Buildbox. It's creating the graphic and audio assets for your games using your favorite graphics and audio software.

Limitations of games based on platforms

When considering what your game will be, it's important to factor the limitations of your target platform into the equation. It seems like forever that Android mobile platforms limited applications to 50 MB in base size (one could make them bigger with extensions, but this could require some extra coding). A 50 MB video game is not very exciting, especially when you consider that a mere 10 minutes of music for such a game would take up around 10 MB or 20% of the game package.

Luckily, in late 2015, the powers that be raised that limitation of the base application (also known as an APK file) to 100 MB. While that's still not a lot by today's standards, it's still plenty for developing an entertaining game. Since Android's limitation is 100 MB—and so is iOS (Apple)—that's what we'll use as our hard limit. However, if we were strictly developing a game for Windows or Macintosh computers, we could ignore this limitation. This brings us to…

The platforms for Buildbox games

Buildbox is pretty amazing in that it can export games for several platforms. As each platform has its own unique intricacies, you can see just how exciting it is that a developer may create one project that exports to several different distribution channels for several platforms. Let's take a quick look:

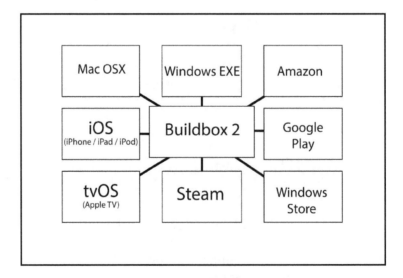

Downloading the color images of this book:
We also provide you with a PDF file that has color graphics of the screenshots/diagrams used in this book. These graphics will help you better understand the changes in the output. You can download this file at the following link: `http://www.packtpub.com/sites/default/files/do` `wnloads/Buildbox2xGameDevelopment_ColorImages.pdf`.

The preceding image shows the various platforms Buildbox 2 is designed to support. Again, with Buildbox, you won't be making the next PlayStation or XBOX FPS. But you can make the next *Flappy Bird* or *Mario Bros*.

The actual process for getting the games onto the various platforms is a bit more complex than the previous image implies. We'll get into the nuts and bolts of the various workflows for export in a later chapter. Suffice it to say, though, that the ability to use one project is definitely a big check mark in the pros column for Buildbox.

You'll notice that there is some duplication of platforms among the various distribution channels (Windows EXE and Steam, or Amazon and Google Play). This is because exporting and some parameters differ between those distribution channels. Confused? Don't worry, we'll clear up the differences between distribution channels and platforms in just a bit.

Defining some terminology

Before we dive into the interface, and dive further into what we're going to cover in this book, let's clear up some terms (such as distribution channels and platforms):

- **Asset**: Any element used in your project. An asset can be anything from a graphic to a sound effect MP3.
- **Project**: The Buildbox file used to create the game.
- **Element:** The use of a visual asset within Buildbox, for example, a button on a menu screen is considered an element.
- **Animation**: The movement of an element within Buildbox.
- **Animated element**: An element consisting of an image sequence giving the appearance of animation, for instance, a running sequence (known as a walk cycle) on the main character to show them running when moving.
- **Physics**: A type of animation within Buildbox allowing movement based on environmental parameters (falling with gravity, bouncing with collisions, and so on).
- **Export**: A set of files generated by Buildbox.

- **Compile**: The act of taking exported files from Buildbox and creating an executable program (or app) from those exported files.
- **Compiler**: Software used to compile.
- **Platform**: A system that will run your compiled program or application, for example, an iOS device or a Windows computer.

- **Distribution channel**: The location where customers will be able to find your compiled game and download it, for example, Google Play, iTunes, Windows Store, Steam, and so on.
- **UI**: The user interface. This includes menus, buttons, score counters, anything the user interacts with or can derive information from.

The equipment and software you'll need

Of course, you should have either a device or emulator for every platform you intend to compile for. An emulator is a piece of software that can mimic a device on the desktop of your computer. You'll need these devices and/or emulators to make sure your app isn't taxing the processing power and memory of a device too much. Although a game could test fine on your desktop, it may prove to be too much for a device to handle.

Additionally, you'll definitely need a Mac of some sort to compile for Apple devices. Unfortunately, the compiler for iOS, tvOS, and Macintosh only runs on Mac. We'll be developing (using Buildbox) on a PC, and compiling for Apple using a Mac Mini for the projects in this book.

To effectively develop a game, you'll also need some sort of image editing software. In this book, we'll be using Adobe Photoshop CC2015 and Illustrator CC2015; however, there are freeware solutions available (such as GIMP—available here: `https://www.gimp.org/downl oads/`).

A worthwhile game absolutely must have good sound. Therefore, a developer must have a decent audio editing application. In this book we'll be using a combination of Presonus Studio One 3 Professional and Adobe Audition CC2015. Again, a freeware option known as Audacity is available from SourceForge at `https://sourceforge.net/projects/audacity /`.

Finally, to create animated assets (such as enemies, explosions, and so on), it's advisable to get a 3D animation program to speed things up. In this book we shall use LightWave 3D 2015; however, yet again, a freeware option known as Blender is available (`https://www.bl ender.org/`).

It is not entirely necessary for a developer to create their own graphic and audio assets. You could always hit up Fiverr (`https://www.fiverr.com/`) or similar services to have custom graphics and audio made for you. However, as this is a complete book on developing a game using Buildbox, we will be covering how to create these assets yourself.

Complete specifications of the development environment

Granted, this greatly exceeds the minimum needed for game development with Buildbox. However, this should give you a good idea of the capabilities necessary, and it's nice to have for game development.

PC (primary development machine)

Processor	Intel I7 5960X
Memory	32 GB 3000Mhz DDR4
Hard drives	512 GB Solid State Boot Drive 10TB RAID 0 SATA II Internal 10TB RAID 1 USB 3.1 External Backup 4TB Seagate Baracuda Docked USB 3.0 Archival Backup
Motion capture (not necessary at all for Buildbox, but helpful for graphics creation)	XBOX One Kinect with USB 3.0 adapter
Color accuracy (not necessary at all for Buildbox, but helpful for graphics creation)	Pantone Huey Pro
Monitor	Samsung 4K oLED
Audio	Presonus FireStudio Project USB 3.0 Interface with Presonus powered speakers
Music hardware	Roland Fantom X6, Roland MC 909, various guitars and basses
Software	Windows 10 Pro x64, Buildbox 2.0, Android SDK 2, Adobe Creative Cloud 2015, LightWave 3D 2015, Brekel Pro motion capture, Presonus Studio One 3 Pro

Mac (for xCode compiling only)

Model	2008 Mac Mini
Operating system	OSX Yosemite
Software	xCode

Distribution channel memberships

Developing a game is only half the picture. Yes, it's cool to be able to play your own games, but wouldn't it be better to have the world play them? Better yet…wouldn't it be better to make a profit? That's where distribution channels come in.

Distribution channels, such as iTunes, Steam, and Google Play, are places where platform owners go to shop for new apps and games. But for each device, there are unique distribution channels, and in some cases multiple ones (such as Google Play and Amazon Apps for Android devices).

In order to develop for Apple devices, you're going to need a subscription to the Apple Developer Program. It is an annual fee, and can be expensive (when compared to Android). Speaking of which, you'll also need a membership to the Google Play developer program, and Amazon developer program.

For Windows games, you will need a Steam account, and to authorize it, to submit programs to *Steam Greenlight*. You will also need a Windows Dev Center account.

As you can see, if you sign up for all of the various services as a developer, the costs can run up. So, it's probably going to be important to make up your mind on the target for your games before you begin developing. The bonus is that if your game does well on one platform, it's very easy to port it to another (because one Buildbox project can generate the same game across multiple platforms).

Tour of the Buildbox interface

Now that we've got a bit of a foundation, let's get into Buildbox itself. We'll spend the rest of this chapter giving you a tour of the Buildbox interface, and in the next chapter we'll go over a template project that comes with Buildbox before creating our own **Ramblin' Rover** game. Alright, here we go…

The welcome screen

When you first open Buildbox, you're greeted with the **Welcome** screen. The following screenshot shows this screen. Buildbox has taken a page straight out of Adobe's UIX design team with this. If this is the first time you've opened the Welcome screen, you should immediately uncheck **Open Buildbox at startup**:

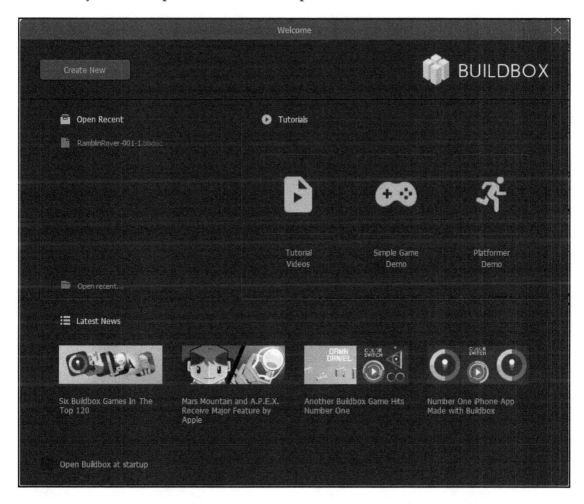

Unless your computer's sole purpose is for Buildbox development, we suggest unchecking this immediately to minimize your frustration upon startup of your computer. For some reason, the Buildbox team believes that everyone would want Buildbox to start every time they restart their computer by default.

Let's take this interface from the bottom up (since we started with the **Open Buildbox at startup** option).

The area near the bottom with the **Latest News** heading is just that. It's the area where you can see what the latest patches and updates are. This is also where you can see how other games made with Buildbox are doing. Clicking these links takes you to the web page(s) where the related stories are.

Just above **Latest News** on the left side of the screen is the **Open Recent** window. It's pretty self-explanatory, but this is where you can easily click on recent Buildbox projects you've been working on to open them.

Now, looking to the right, we see the **Tutorials** section. This is where you can check out some examples and videos on how to use Buildbox. Let's take a look at these one by one:

- **Tutorial Videos**: By clicking this, you'll be taken to a page on the Buildbox website that hosts several videos showing how to use various aspects of the Buildbox software
- **Sample Game Demo**: This will open a very rudimentary game demo with some text overlays to give you a high level overview of the development environment
- **Platformer Demo**: Clicking on this option will open another rudimentary game demo showing off some of the features of developing a platformer-style video game

Finally, there is the **Create New** button on the top-left of the screen. This is exactly what it sounds like. It will enable you to create a new project by launching the **Creator** screen. This brings us to…

The Creator screen

Welcome to the **Creator** screen (shown in the following screenshot). This is where you'll set up your basic parameters for a new game. Let's take a look at these parameters one by one.

In the **Name** field, you can type in a plain English name for your project. This actually has no bearing on the final game, it's really just a name for your project.

Basic settings

Looking down and to the left, we have the **Basic Settings** of a game. Inside, we have the **Orientation**, and **Score Type** settings. **Orientation** lets you determine whether a game will be **Landscape** (wide screen) or **Portrait** (tall screen). If you're developing a computer game, this should almost always be **Landscape**. Some examples of game types that might use **Portrait** are an avoidance or zig-zag type game on mobile devices (we'll define these better in just a bit).

The next setting is the **Score Type**. This will depend on the type of game you're using, and your monetization model. There are three basic types of scoring in Buildbox:

- **Distance**: Just as it sounds, this scoring is based on how far you travel in the game. Motocross, avoidance, zig-zag, and even some platformers (among others) use this type of scoring.
- **Coins Collected**: Think of Nintendo's *Super Mario Bros.* here. A typical platformer game will give you score based on the number and type (some pickups being worth more coins than others) of coins collected.
- **Points Collected**: If you're planning on instituting a Coin Store but want a scoring style similar to *Super Mario Bros.*, you'd want to use this scoring motif. You can assign points to objects in parallel with coins (for example, collecting an object may be worth 10 points, and 1 coin). This way, users can compete against other users with score, and still purchase items in the Coin Store without affecting their score balance.

As alluded to in the **Points Collected** bullet, your **Score Type** is an important setting because this is how players will be able to measure their performance against others. Yes, you may implement leaderboards (on most platforms) that are web-enabled to spur competition among users. When designing a game, your scoring method should be one of the first things you consider.

Gameplay settings

This is probably the most important setting selection on this screen. The **Gameplay Type** drop-down menu sets up the template for your whole game. As described, this is where you set what type of game you'll create. Let's take a quick look at the types of games in the stock templates(we'll get deeper into these in *Chapter 8, Building Other Popular Game Types*):

- `Default`: This template is a kind of bouncy ball game that allows you to move a character to the left and right (as well as slow the descent of the ball).

- 360 Shooter: Think *Asteroids* with this template. Here, you can create a game where a spaceship turns 360 degrees, avoids obstacles, and shoots others.
- Around the World: Here, you can create a game where you're fighting the orbital gravity of a planet while avoiding obstacles.
- Avoidance: A constantly scrolling game where you must move your character to avoid obstacles.
- Dog Fight: For this, think *Spyhunter* or *Gallaga*. Similar to the *360 Shooter*, but your gun is pointing in one direction. You must avoid obstacles and kill enemies.
- Downward Bounce: Another bouncy ball game. But instead of merely slowing the descent of your ball, you can dribble it like a basketball.
- Fall Buttons: Here, you guide a character as it falls down through a series of objects. You can use left/right controls to influence your character as gravity makes it fall.
- Fall Switch: Almost the same as Fall Buttons, but instead you have a single button control that simply switches the direction (left or right) of your character. Much more fast-paced.
- Flappy: Just like it sounds, think *Flappy Bird* or *Drone Challenge*. Here you guide your character through obstacles using *Joust*-style flapping controls to keep your character in the air.
- Gravity Portal: This is kind of a mind-bender. Here your game will have two game fields: one the right way up and one upside down. On tapping the screen, the character will fly up off screen, and return coming up through the bottom.
- Gravity Runner: Similar to Gravity Portal, except instead of going off screen, you have a ceiling and floor. A tap of the screen makes the ceiling the gravity source and tapping it again changes gravity back to the floor.
- Impossible: This is kind of a platformer game. However, you cannot stop, nor reverse direction. The game keeps you moving and you must jump to avoid obstacles.
- ISO Jump Slide: Isometric (2.5D) game where you jump over some obstacles and slide under others.
- ISO Jump: Almost exactly the same. Here, you can jump, but not slide through a constantly moving Isometric field.
- Jetpack: Think *Jetpack Joyride* with this. Very similar to *Flappy*.
- Jumping: Here, you guide a character through a vertical world using a flap-style jump control while avoiding obstacles.

- `Motocross`: A vehicle side-scroller where you guide a vehicle over various obstacles while doing flips.

- `Platformer`: Truly the *Super Mario Bros.* experience. You guide your character and jump over obstacles to collect coins and points.
- `Racing`: A top-view racing game where you must avoid other cars while the game vertically scrolls.
- `Runner`: Like *Jetpack* on the ground, you must avoid obstacles by jumping. You can move backward, but don't go too far!
- `Shooting Runner`: Just like `Runner` with the addition of guns to shoot enemies.
- `Side Shooter`: Same exact game as `360 Shooter` without the ability to turn your gun to shoot in other directions.
- `Stage Clear`: *Pac-Man* style game where you must collect everything/destroy all enemies to win the stage.
- `Sticky Jump`: Here, you jump to avoid obstacles as you would in a platformer. However, the game only scrolls while you are in the air.
- `Wall Jump`: In this game, the screen scrolls vertically, and gravity is on one side. You have to move left and right to avoid obstacles by jumping to the other side, or letting your character fall to the gravity wall.
- `Wall Reverse`: A strange type of game that is a combination of Jetpack and Wall Jump. You just use arrows and jump to get your character to a goal object.
- `Zig-Zag`: This type of game is a combination of Wall Jump and Gravity Runner. Think of it as a vertical version of Gravity Runner.

Now that we've outlined all of the game types that Buildbox has to offer, we still advise you to go take a look at them one by one. You really have to experience them to fully understand them. You can also combine types of games by adding other elements and rules as we'll do in *Ramblin' Rover*, which will be a combination of a motocross, a platformer, and a shooting runner.

World settings

Don't confuse the **Game Type** drop-down menu here with the **Gameplay Type** drop-down menu in **Gameplay Settings**. The **Game Type** drop-down menu lets you select whether this game will have a single world, or many unique worlds. A unique world will have a different background, can have different obstacles, characters, and even different physics parameters.

The `World End Action` parameter allows you to further define the structure of your game by choosing whether your game will be endless (repeat scenes within a world at random endlessly) or have an end scene once a goal is reached.

Menu settings

This area has checkboxes for **Pause**, **Game Over**, **Coin Shop** and **Info**, and allows you to set up what other interfaces you'd like to include.

For instance, checking the **Pause** option will create a unique screen that will appear when a user pauses the game. An **Info** screen can be used to give credits to your staff, instructions for gameplay, or anything you can think of that fits in no other category. And a **Coin Shop** is an area that will allow users to buy more coins to unlock other characters and abilities within the game.

The world editor

The image below shows the world editor. As a Buildbox developer, this is where you'll spend most of your time. It also happens to be the most fun screen in Buildbox. A world consists of many scenes in Buildbox. They all share the same backgrounds and characters. Let's start with the scene editor:

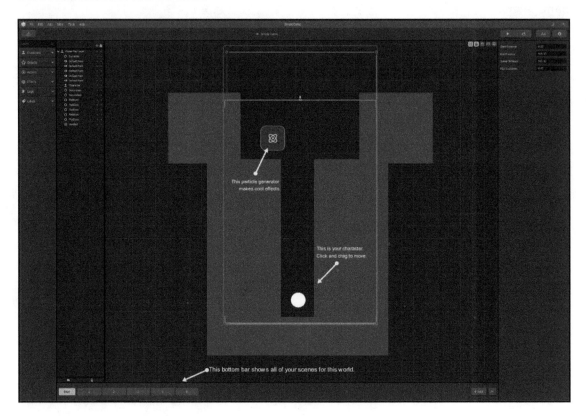

The scene editor

In the following , you can see that we have a start scene, as well as an additional five scenes. Editing is easy: just click the scene you'd like to edit, and work with it:

On the right side of the scene editor, you'll notice the **+ Add** button, and the ^ button. The **+ Add** button allows you to add a blank scene to your world (although you can also duplicate the currently selected scene with the keyboard shortcut of *D* for duplicate.) The ^ button opens the timeline editor:

As you can see in the image above, this timeline plays each scene sequentially. However, you could overlap scenes, or even have them all run in parallel. This type of layout enables the scenes to be played in random order, giving the player a unique experience every time they play. The parallel layout is optimal for endless games, while the sequential layout is best for goal-oriented games.

The game field (the stage)

The game field (shown in the following screenshot) is where you'll actually build your scenes. Here, you can add objects, text, background graphics, decorations, and all kinds of effects and logic elements. On the left side of the game field, you'll see the layer editor (Outliner), which enables you to bring objects forward or back, select objects easily, hide, or even lock them. This area greatly helps keep your scene organized:

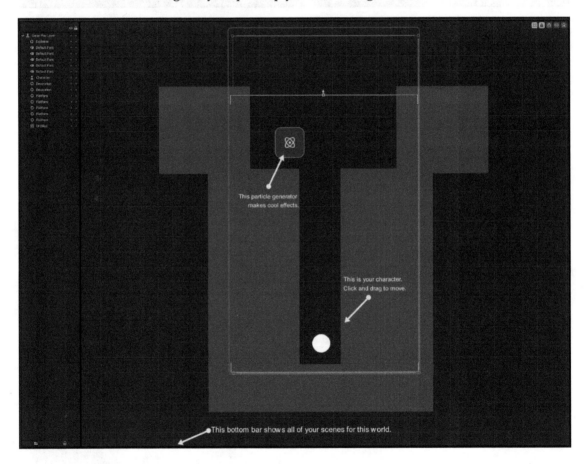

On the upper-right you have various display options for the game field, viz:

- **Show Game Field**: This shows where your character can travel and sets boundaries (barriers and lethal barriers) for it:

- **Lock Backgrounds**: Locking backgrounds prevents you from accidentally shifting them when moving other objects around on your stage:

- **Snap Movement**: This lets objects *snap* to a grid or other objects as you move them around on your stage:

- **Activate Connection Mode**: By activating connection mode, you can connect (parent) objects to other objects (for example, if you apply physics, this will help you make swinging laps):

- **Apply Debug Mode**: In Debug mode, you can see collision shapes. This will allow you to make sure objects have proper shapes, and ensure that your game is playable:

Object parameters

On the right side of the screen, you'll find the parameters area. This will show (and enable you to edit) parameters for any selected object. Currently, the start scene is selected, so what is showing right now are the parameters for the start scene in our example (as shown in the following screenshot):

The library

On the far left you'll notice the library window. Here is where all of your objects are kept for you to use. They are grouped by type. The following screenshot shows the library window:

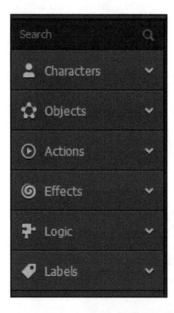

Once you import an object once, you only need to find it into the library. Importing an object twice is not advisable (as it creates a duplicate of the same asset, and can use up more resources than necessary). Instead, come to the library and find it. Here are the categories and what they mean:

- **Characters**: Objects that the user controls. This is like Mario in *Super Mario Bros*.
- **Objects**: These are any non-character, and non-action objects such as platforms, obstacles, decorations, and enemies.
- **Actions**: Action objects are things such as coin and point pickups.
- **Effects**: These come in very handy. Effects include particle emitters, flags, and trails. They can add a bit more punch to your look. Be careful, though. They can be resource intensive.
- **Logic**: Here is where you'll find tools to make your game more interesting. Hidden level teleports, portals, even character multipliers (cloning your character) can be found here.
- **Labels**: Labels are merely text objects you can throw onto your stage. They can be quite useful to help with instruction during a training world, or to add statements such as *Start* or *WATCH OUT!* to your game.

Additional buttons

At the upper-right of your screen, you'll see four buttons that are very useful. Let's take them from left to right:

- **Preview**: This button allows you to try out your game using the game preview screen. We'll show you this screen at the end of this chapter.
- **Preview Current Scene**: By previewing only the current scene, you can skip to what is relevant to what you're working on.
- **Font Editor**: Fonts in Buildbox must be packaged with your final compiled game. This will allow you to add fonts from your computer to the game. We'll save this screen for a later chapter.

- **Game Settings**: This screen allows you to set up your game for export by adjusting parameters such as the game's icon, build ID, and various advertising and monetization settings. We'll save this screen for a later chapter.

Finally, at the upper-left of the screen, you'll notice this button. This button will close your world and bring you to the **Game Mind Map**.

The Game Mind Map

The image below shows the Game Mind Map of our basic game. This screen is where you can edit the structure of your game. As you'll also notice, as our world is selected, you can edit the parameters of the world in the parameter window:

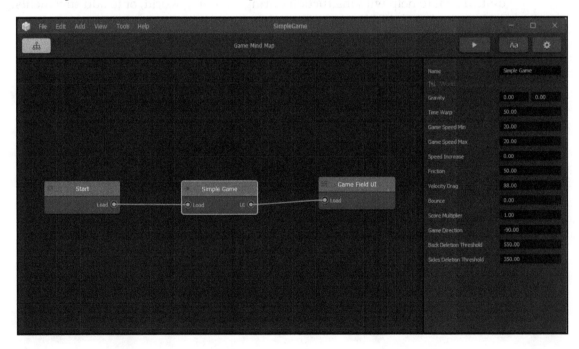

This is how you change the gravity settings for individual worlds to give a wider spectrum of user experience to your players. This is a simple game (and is aptly titled). Let's take a look at what Ramblin' Rover will look like when it's near completion:

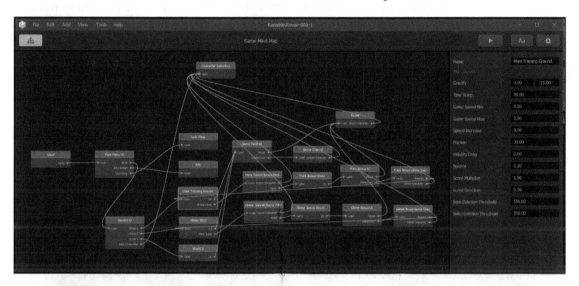

Here, you can see why a node-based editor for the structure of a game is important. This is Ramblin' Rover with the first two of the three worlds we'll create completed. Don't feel overwhelmed. By the end of this book, this screen will look extremely simple to you. I invite you to come back and look at it once you've completed the book to see just how far you've come!

The Atlas screen

All graphics assets in Buildbox are handled as sprites via an atlas. Confused? Don't worry, we will get deeper into the atlas editor in a later chapter. For now, we just wanted to make you aware that this editor exists. This is considered an advanced screen, so be patient. We will cover this later:

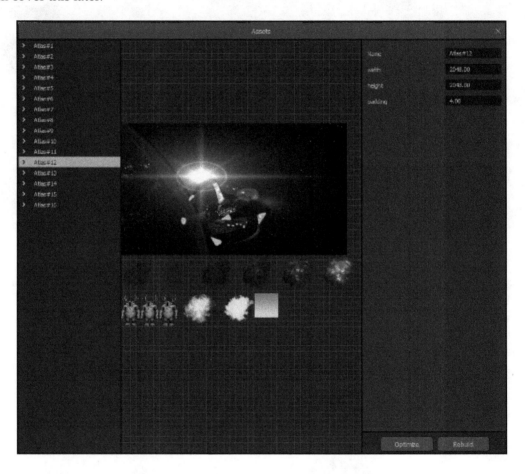

The Game Preview screen

This is the most gratifying interface in Buildbox. The following image shows the Game Preview interface:

This is where you can actually play and test your game. You may recognize the **Debug Mode** button on the upper-left of the interface. This will let you actually play the game while viewing all your connections and collision shapes. Very useful indeed.

Also on the screen is a screenshot button, which will let you save screenshots of your game for later (quite useful for when you go to put your game on a distribution channel). You can also emulate the resolutions on various devices using the drop-down menu (currently at **1920×1080 Full HD**) and another drop-down menu allows you to scale the percentage to blow up the image or shrink it.

If you have multiple monitors, or a monitor with a high enough resolution, you can always leave this window open, and when you want to play your game with any changes you made, just hit the **Refresh** button (upper-right).

Summary

In this chapter, you've learned about setting up your development environment, the capabilities of Buildbox, and you've even gotten a tour of the interface. There's still a lot to learn before we dive head first into the Ramblin' Rover project. So, in the next chapter we're going to take a closer look at some of the procedures of Buildbox so you can gain some familiarity with the methodologies within the software using the Platformer Demo from the tutorials section on the Welcome screen.

Ready to take a look at this example project before we dive into making Ramblin' Rover? Let's do this!

2
Orientation

Now that you've seen the Buildbox interface, and had a bit of an introduction to the world of game development, let's take a quick look at how things are done inside Buildbox. Let's begin by opening the **Platformer Demo** from the **Welcome Screen**.

Using the Game Mind Map

Upon opening the **Platformer Demo**, you'll be confronted with the game stage. Let's click the **Game Mind Map** button (top-left of the screen) to check it out:

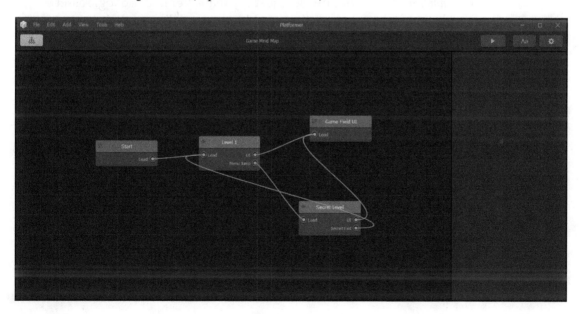

The Game Mind Map is where you can change the user experience of your game. It's also how you navigate to each area you'd like to edit.

This type of interface is known as a *node-based interface*. Essentially, it's an interactive flowchart. The individual blocks are called nodes. Lines come into nodes on the left and exit on the right. Let's take a minute and go over the nodes for this example game.

- All games start with a `Start` node. Think of this as a splash screen where you can show your logo, and add a loading bar (the status of the game loading into memory) while the rest of the game's loading is completed. Once loading is finished, the user will be taken directly into Level 1.
- The `Level 1` node, you'll notice, is blue. Blue nodes are worlds and green nodes are user interface (UI) nodes. You'll also see that the `Level 1` node has two outputs on its right side.
- The `UI` output is fairly self-explanatory. This is where you select a screen to be overlaid on your world. This UI screen may contain your score, controls, and even event handlers, such as a *Game Over* handler to send someone to a new screen if their character dies.
- The `Menu Jump` output on the right of the `Level 1` node is tied to a node called *Secret Level*. This is because somewhere in the `Level 1` world, a `Menu Jump` logic asset has been placed. We'll get deeper into what these logic assets are when we develop *Ramblin' Rover*. For now, let's just say that a `Menu Jump` logic asset allows a player to teleport to another world (or menu UI) once their character touches the asset in the game field.
- You might also notice that both of the worlds (`Level 1` and `Secret Level`) use the same `Game Field UI` node. It makes sense if you consider it. All this means is that both worlds use the same interface overlay.

Now, what if we wanted to add a *Game Over* screen to this game?

Making a game over screen

This exercise will show you how to make some connections and new nodes using the Game Mind Map.

The first thing we're going to want is an event listener to sense when a character dies. It sounds complex, and if we were coding a game, this would take several lines of code to accomplish. In Buildbox, it's a simple drag-and-drop method.

If you double-click on the **Game Field UI** node, you'll be presented with the overlay for the UI and controls during gameplay. Since this is a basic template, you are actually presented with a blank screen. This template is for you to play around with on a computer, so no controls are on the screen. Instead, it is assumed that you would use keyboard controls to play the demo game. This is why the screen looks blank:

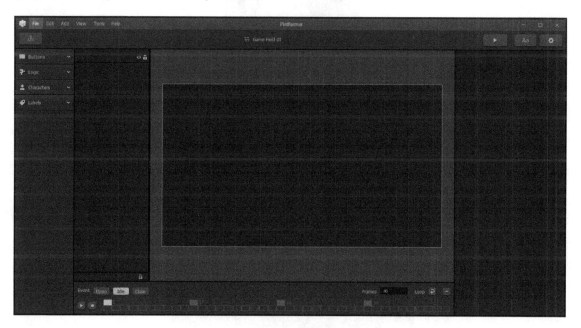

There are some significant differences between the UI editor and the World editor. You can notice that the **Character** tab from the asset library is missing and there is a timeline editor on the bottom. We'll get into how to use this timeline later. For now, let's keep things simple and add our **Game Over** sensor:

If you expand the **Logic** tab in the asset library, you'll find the **Event Observer** object. You may drag this object anywhere onto the stage. It doesn't even have to be in the visible window (the dark area in the center of the stage). So long as it's somewhere on the stage, the game can use this logic asset. If you do put it on the visible area of the stage, don't worry; it's an invisible asset, and won't show in your game:

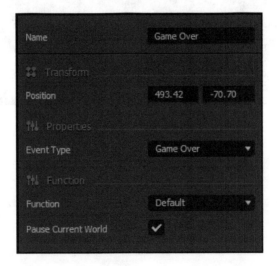

While the **Event Observer** is selected on the stage, you'll notice that its properties pop up in the properties window (on the right side of the screen). By default, the **Game Over** type of event is selected. But if you select this drop-down menu, you'll notice a ton of different event types that this logic asset can handle. Let's leave all of the properties at their default values (except the name; please change this to **Game Over**) and go back to the **Game Mind Map** (top-left button):

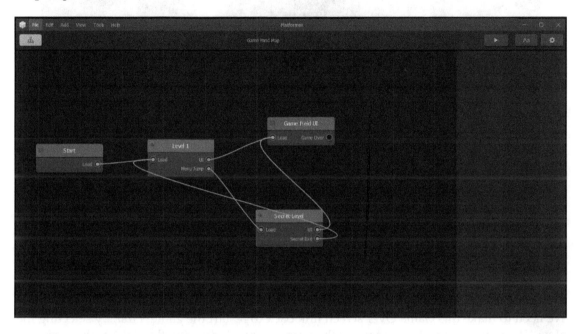

Do you notice anything different? The **Game Field UI** node now has a **Game Over** output. Now, we just need a place to send that output.

Right-click on the blank space of the grid area. Now you can either create a new world or new UI. Select **Add New UI** and you'll see a new green node that is titled **New UI1**. This new UI will be your Game Over screen when a character dies.

Before we can use this new node, it needs to be connected to the **Game Over** output of the **Game Field UI**. This process is exceedingly simple. Just hold down your left mouse button on the **Game Over** output's dark dot, and drag to the **New UI1**'s Load dark dot (on the left side of the **New UI1** node).

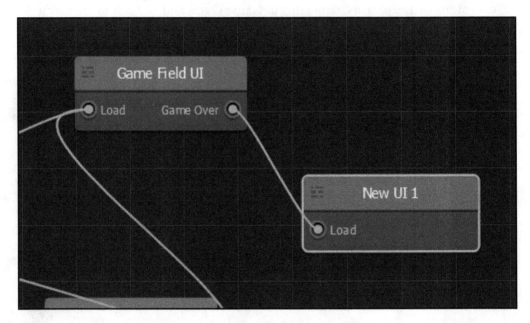

Congratulations, you've just created your first connected node. We're not done yet, though. We need to make this Game Over screen link back to restart the game. First, by selecting the **New UI1** node, change its name using the parameters window (on the right of the screen) to **Game Over** UI. Make sure you hit your Enter key; this will commit the changed name. Now double-click on the Game Over UI node so we can add some elements to the screen.

You can't have a Game Over screen without the words Game Over, so let's add some text:

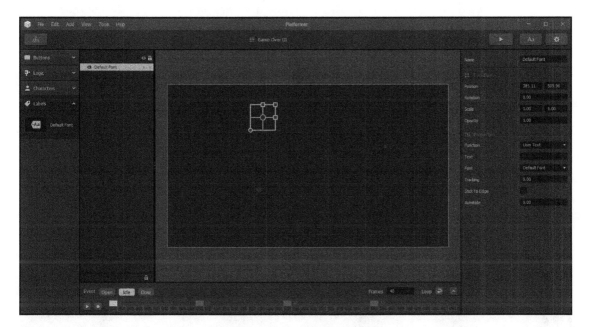

The preceding screenshot shows a label asset applied to the screen. This is where it will eventually say Game Over. Under the **Labels** section of the asset library, you'll see a **Default Font** asset. Drag this asset to the visible grid (the darker area) of the stage and you should see a green cursor with a blue adjustment box around it. Notice that no text is in the area yet.

In the Text field of the properties window on the right side of the screen, type *Game Over*. After you hit *Enter*, you'll notice that your text now appears on the screen. Resize that (using the handle on the upper-right of the blue box around the text) to a large size, and you should have something like this:

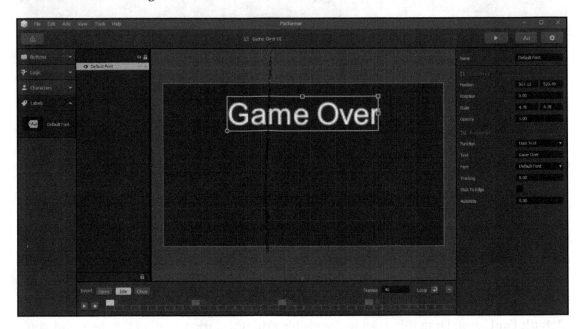

Before we move on, tick the checkbox next to **Stick To Edge** in the properties window. This keeps the text's relationship to the nearest edge of the visible area (which is handy when you compile for different platforms that have different resolutions).

Well, this looks…really boring. We need text that *pops* more. Now we'll take a quick look at how to change the fonts for your game.

Changing your game fonts

As promised in the last chapter, we're about to show you the fonts interface. You could have the most beautiful graphics and audio possible in your game. Without a font that ties it all together and goes well with your graphics…well, you're just not going to make your players happy.

When choosing fonts, you should think about the mood of your game, the genre, and the era you're portraying. For example, you wouldn't choose a heavy technical-looking font for something taking place in the Wild West (unless of course, you're going for steampunk). Needless to say, font choice is extremely important, and probably the most overlooked asset in mobile and indie games today.

Let's get to it. If you click on the **Font Editor** button (top-right corner of the screen…the **Aa** button), the Font Editor window will open.

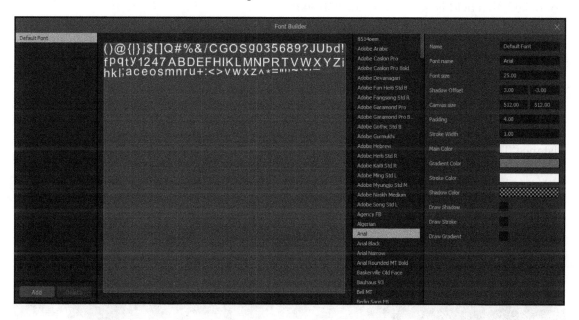

The preceding image shows the **Font Editor** (the Font Builder). Here, you can make just about any font look good. Let's stay basic (with Arial) so you can see just what a difference some embellishments and a better resolution can make.

On the Game Over screen, we made the font so much bigger that it blurred and pixelated. First off, let's create a new font for our Game Over text. By clicking on the **Add** button on the lower left, a new font is created (currently called **Untitled Font**). In the **Name** field of the properties window, change the name to Large Text. It's important to name your objects as you go to minimize confusion down the line. A full game will end up quite complex, and you definitely want to keep up good organization and naming conventions.

In the properties window, shift the **Font Size** up to 75.0. Now we can have big fonts that are nice and clear. We should also make this font nice and contrasty and colorful. We also want to make this font visible (no matter the brightness or color of the background).

You may notice that this font has a gradient applied to it (because the **Draw Gradient** checkbox is ticked). The **Main Color** field will change the color at the top of the font when the **Draw Gradient** checkbox is ticked. When it's not ticked, this will make the entire font this color. Let's change the **Main Color** to bright yellow. You can do this by clicking on its current color (a large grey box currently) which will bring up a color selector window.

Now, we shall change the bottom color of the font using the **Gradient Color** field. Go ahead and change it to a dark red. It should be noted that when the **Draw Gradient** checkbox is not ticked, this field is ignored by the software.

Now we need to make sure that the font is readable on both dark and light backgrounds. We'll do this using both stroke and shadow. Tick both **Draw Shadow** and **Draw Stroke**, and change the **Stroke Color** to pure black. You may notice that the shadow is projected up and to the right. It's also pretty close to the lettering.

To change this, all we really have to do is change the **Shadow Offset**. The first number (currently at 3.00) is the horizontal distance, and the second number (-3.00) is the vertical distance. The fact that the vertical distance is negative is why the shadow is up. If the horizontal number were negative, it would go left (rather than right). Let's set both numbers to 4.0 (which will make the shadow down and to the right). Now that you're done, things should look something like this:

Now you can see how just a little bit of work can make even a boring font like Arial look good and rich. Go ahead and close the **Font Editor** window.

So, why does the *Game Over* text still look the same? Because we didn't change the default font. Instead, we created a new one for large text. We can assign our new Large Text font pretty easily. First, select the Game Over text by clicking on it. The first thing we should remember is that the default font was really small. So, before we change the font, let's change the scale to 2.0. This can be done in the properties window. There, you'll find the **Scale** fields. Whenever you see two text fields next to each other, this will be the same as the **Shadow** fields from the **Font Editor** (where the first field is horizontal, and the second is vertical). So, just change both fields to 2.0.

Now, in the properties window, look for the **Font** drop-down menu. In this, select the **Large Text** font we created. The result should look like this:

Now, we'll create a button to restart the game…

Setting up a navigation button

Using your asset library, open up the **Buttons** section and drag a **Navigation Button** to the visible area of the stage. Rename this button**Restart** using the **Name** field of the parameters window.

In the interest of time, we'll borrow some of our assets from Ramblin' Rover. If you haven't downloaded the free content yet, you can always create a quick button in your graphics program. Make it 300 x 100, and it must be saved as a PNG file. PNG files are the only graphics assets that Buildbox will accept. We'll get further into graphics while we are making Ramblin' Rover in a later chapter. If you have the content, we'll open up a file browser to where you extracted the content. We'll be using `Projects/RamblinRover/Buttons/RESTART.png`.

Now that we have a browser window open to where the button graphic is held and we have the **Navigation Button** asset on our stage, drag the image file from your browser, and drop it into the **Image** field of the properties window for your restart button in Buildbox. The result should look something like this:

We could simplify the process a bit by changing the **Function** drop-down menu from **Default** to **Restart**. However, as this game has a secret level, we wouldn't want to simply restart the hidden level if the character dies. Instead, we want to restart from the beginning of the original world. So instead, we're going to leave this as **Default** (which will create a new output node for the **Game Over UI**). So let's go back to the **Game Mind Map**.

Just as we did when we joined the **Game Over** output from the **Game Field UI** to the **Game Over UI**'s **Load** input, we'll drag a line from the `Restart` output on the **Game Over UI** to the **Load** input on the **Level 1** node. And there you have it, your Game Over screen is all done! It should look like this:

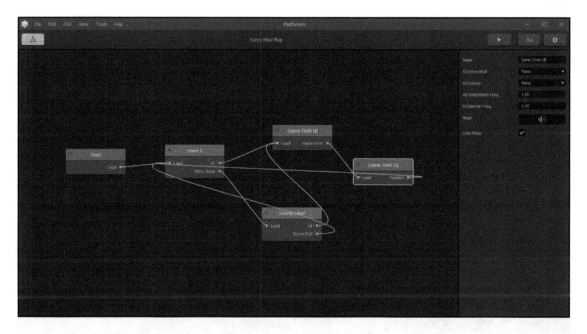

Congratulations! Your game is now playable. Click on the **Preview** button at the top right of the screen and give it a whirl.

Altering the template game

Ok…so it's a little slow and boring. So, let's get into making it a bit more exciting. Start by speeding things up. Select the **Level 1** node, and increase the **Time Warp** value to 100 (currently set at 55). This will nearly double the speed of the game making it more challenging and fun. Give it a try now (using the **Preview** button). So, even though the graphics are still boring and primitive, you actually begin to have some fun.

This is a great example of what world parameters can do. Simply changing one parameter can give the player an entirely different game experience. We'll be using this principle heavily with Ramblin' Rover. The player will have the chance to drive their rover on several different planets. Using parameters, we can change whether the wheels spin out on a vehicle, how much pull the gravity has, and even how much the atmosphere drags when you perform tricks.

But we digress…let's go make this thing look a bit better too. Start by double-clicking on the **Level 1** node…

Working with graphic assets

Although this is a tutorial demo, this is very close to what the Buildbox templates look like upon loading; grey obstacles and assets with a white character. All are primitives. It's actually pretty smart if you consider it. This makes it easy to tell what assets still need to be replaced when creating a game.

Let's start off by turning off all of the buttons at the top-right of the stage (ShowGameFrame, LockBackground, and ActivateConnectionMode). We'll turn some of these back on later, but for now they're obstructing our view. Let's also get rid of all the tutorial text objects and arrows in our frame by selecting them with your mouse and hitting *Delete* on your keyboard. Now your screen should look something like the following screenshot:

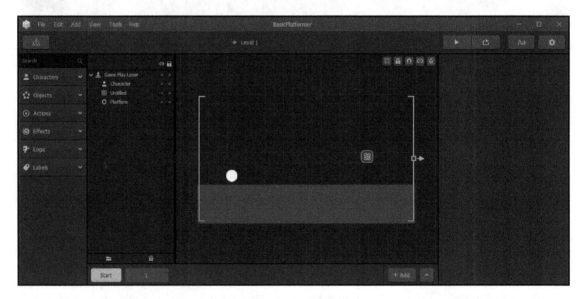

Now, let's replace the most prominent graphic asset in the game... the character. With this small exercise, you're learning the basics of Buildbox. Let's kill two birds with one stone here; we'll also learn about image sequence animations.

We've created a small 15-frame animation of a pair of eyes with shoes that we'll dub Herman. There are two types of animation in Buildbox:

- Where an asset is moved across the screen using keyframes. We'll get into this type of animation later.
- Where an asset itself has several different images (also called frames) to create the illusion of movement, kind of like a flip-book or a film strip.

The image below shows all 15 frames from Herman's walk cycle. A walk cycle animation is a series of images that can be looped to create what looks like a character walking on a treadmill. In cartoons, this walk cycle would be then moved across a background (the first type of animation). Since it's our character, we'll set this up so that whenever it moves, this walk cycle plays:

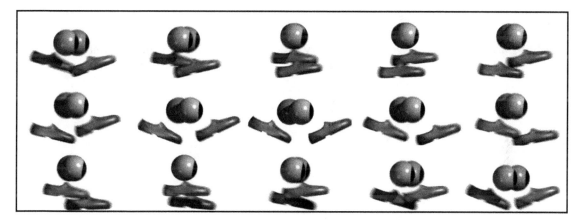

You may notice that it's just Herman taking two steps. But because the last frame of the animation leads into the first, it's loopable. The actual character we'll need is only around 80-90 pixels tall. But since we may play this on large devices (such as a Windows computer with a 4K monitor), we've rendered (output the animation from our 3D software) at twice the resolution we needed (300 x 175).

If you've downloaded the content, you can find these images in `Projects/BasicPlatformer/Characters/Herman`. In the asset library, open the **Characters** section and click on the image of the white-ball character. This will open the properties for the character itself. It's different than clicking on the character on the stage. When selecting the character on the stage, you will edit its *instance* properties. An instance is a single use of an object from the asset library. When selecting the object inside the asset library, the *global* properties of that object are available. Global properties affect every instance of the object everywhere in the game.

Applying image-sequence animations to objects is fairly easy. All graphics assets in Buildbox pretty much work the same way...drag and drop. Do you remember how we created the **Restart** button on the Game Over screen? We just dragged the image over and dropped it on an image field.

Applying animated image sequences is very much the same thing. Where a character is different than a button is that it's made up of several image sequence animations:

The image on the right shows the properties for the (currently) white ball character. First, let's change the **Name** to Herman.

If you select all of the images from the walk cycle image sequence, you can simply drag them (all at the same time...not individually) to the **Move Animation** field.

Now try the game using the **Preview** button. When Herman is standing still, he's a small ball. When you move him, he's a huge character...but he walks. Granted, the graphic of him walking is not aligned to the ground (yet), and he's way too big...but he walks! We'll fix his size and alignment soon. For now, let's get some more animations set up.

In your file browser, locate `Projects/BasicPlatformer/Characters/Herman-Idle`. Select all of the images from this folder and drag them to the `Default Animation` field.

Then, drag all of the images from the `Projects/BasicPlatformer/Characters/Herman-Jump` folder to the **Jump Animation** field. The result should look something like the following screenshot:

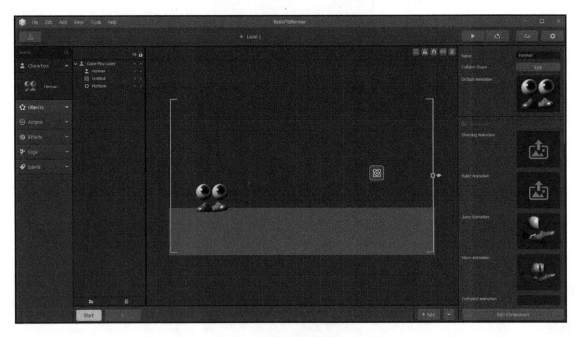

Now that an ugly white ball has been transformed into an actual character, we need to make that character right for our world. First, we have to alter Herman's Collision Shape. Currently, the software still thinks that Herman is a small ball and not a large character with other shapes. So if we were to play the game right now, his feet would be below the ground and he would even seem to go through objects. Open the **Collision Shape Editor** window by clicking on the **Edit** button of the **Collision Shape** field. You should now see the **Shape Editor** window, and it will resemble the following screenshot:

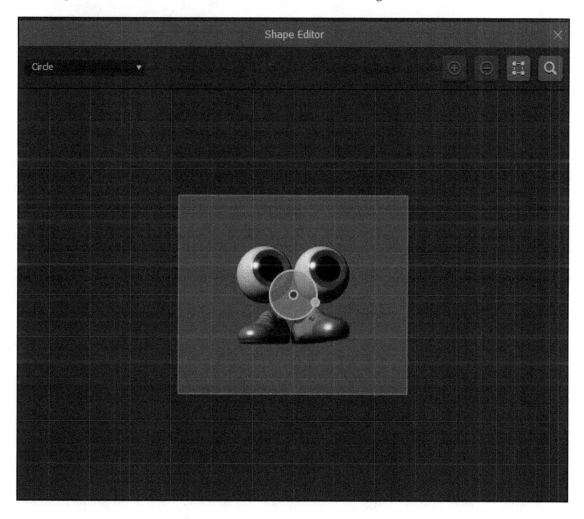

The orange circle in the center is the current collision shape. Let's change it to a polygon by selecting Polygon from the drop-down menu in the upper-left of the window.

You should now see a square, but we need a more complex shape. By clicking the + icon on the top-left of the window, you can add points to the polygon. You'll want to add two points, and drag the points until the resemble they next screenshot:

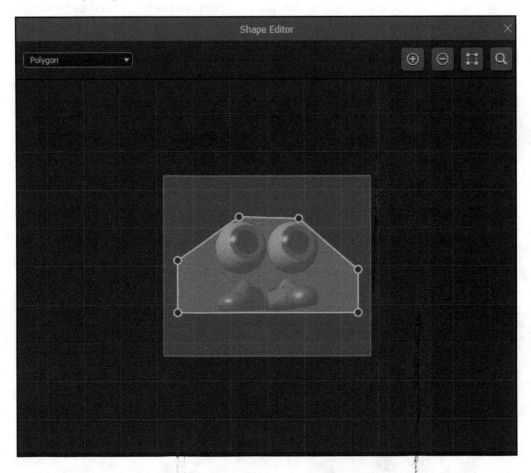

You may wonder why this shape is wider than the actual image. Well, that's because we have to account for the walk cycle's feet moving while Herman walks. Notice that we also lined up the bottom of the collision shape with the bottom of Herman's feet. If (while dragging points around) you see the shape turn red, this means it is not a usable shape. Buildbox does not allow concave areas of a collision shape. If it turns red, just move the points until the shape turns orange again, remembering that any areas of the shape must be convex. Do you feel like you're back in high school geometry yet? See, it wasn't a useless class!

We'll get much deeper into collision shapes when we make Ramblin' Rover. Remember, the purpose of this chapter is to just give you a feel for how Buildbox works at a high level. We'll drill down into the details as we go.

Now, let's make Herman the right size and position him. Close the **Shape Editor** window. After selecting Herman on the stage, set both**Scale** fields to a value of 0.5. Then, drag him so that his feet are hovering just over the ground (not in contact, but just above). When the game starts, he'll drop down to the ground. The following screenshot shows Herman at the correct scale, and placed properly:

Give it a try using the **Preview** button. Now we've gone from a boring white ball to a cute character that the player can identify with.

If you play the game, you'll notice that although we removed the text and arrows, they pop up again downstream. This is because we haven't removed them from the other scene just yet.

Working with scenes

Scenes are just sections of a world chained together. They are the essence of how a game is structured in Buildbox. By using scenes, you can set up a game to play them sequentially, set them up to play randomly (to change the game to a unique experience whenever played), and even make them a rare find by using a cooldown time.

At the bottom of the screen, you'll see the Scene Selection interface. Currently, the `Start` scene is selected. By clicking on the button with the number `1` in it, we will be able to edit that scene. Once you have clicked it, you should be able to delete all of the arrows and text from this scene, following the same procedure as before.

Moving around on the stage is a bit clunky in Buildbox. Currently, you may not be able to see the entire stage. By holding down the spacebar, you can drag the scene around to see all of the areas of it. Also, you can zoom in and out by simply using the scroll-wheel of your mouse. Use these controls to make sure you've removed all the arrows and text, then focus in on the stack of blocks.

You should be where the image below indicates. Since we changed our **Time Warp** setting for this world, it has affected the physics. The block wall that used to fall over now ends up on the ground before we get to it. Let's go ahead and stack the blocks a bit better:

Start by deleting all of the stacked blocks except the bottom one. We're about to learn about instancing. Now that you have only one block to worry about, position this block directly on the ground. This is done by zooming in on it as far as possible, and using your arrow keys to move the object down until there is no gap under it. Be careful not to go further than the ground though, as this can cause issues. Your result should look like this:

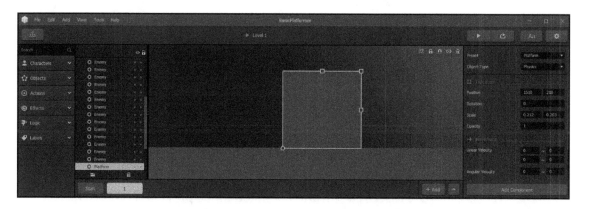

Now for the easy part. Start by zooming out with your **Mouse Wheel** so you can see the floor and ceiling (as well as the box you just positioned). With the block still selected, hit your W key on the keyboard five times. You now have six blocks all stacked on each other. The instancing controls are the same as *W, A, S* and *D* controls in a video game. *W* instances objects up, *A* instances objects to the left, *S* instances objects down, and *D* instances objects to the right. The following screenshot shows your wall aligned more nicely, and prepared for the new physics settings:

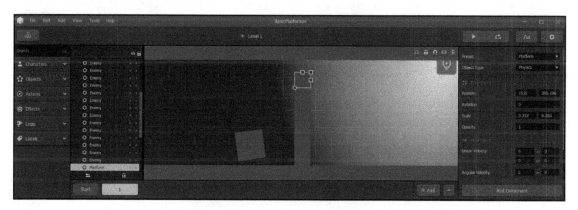

There's just one more thing we need to do in order to make this functional. Our old character had a much smaller collision shape. Before, the big block would activate when we got close and knock down the wall. Since our collision shape is bigger, the center of our character can't activate the block easily. This is what's known as a *wake-up distance*.

Select the larger block to the left of the wall, and in the Properties window, change the **Wake Up Distance** to 150. This should give us enough space so that the block knocks down the wall easier. Give the game a try!

You might notice that once you go to the secret level, things move slowly again, and Herman is HUGE! This is because each world has different settings for physics. Each world is really a separate game all in itself.

Working with worlds

Although worlds can share assets, each world (as stated in the previous sections) has its own physics. It also has a unique background. This way, each world is just that...a world unique all unto itself. But we really have a world that is supposed to mirror the previous world because it's just a secret area. So, we have to really mimic all of the same settings we input for the Level 1 world.

Try to remember what we did to the physics settings and to the size settings. If you can, go repeat this process from memory. If not, here is how it is done again.

Go back to the Game Mind Map. Here, click the **SecretLevel** node to select it. Once the **Secret Level** node is selected, set the **TimeWarp** setting (in the Properties window) to 100.

Now that we've matched the physics up so they're cohesive, let's set up Herman to match the Level 1 world. Double-click the **Secret Level** node to open up that world. You're going to want to make sure that the **Start** scene is the scene that is selected. The reason is that the character can only be edited in the Start scene. In all other scenes, just a ghost of the character shows on the stage.

Change both of the Scale values for Herman to 0.5. Also, navigate between the two scenes and make sure any text and arrows are deleted.

And there you have it! You now have a playable game (granted, it's very simple and rudimentary), and you should be proud. After all, it's one more game you've built with Buildbox than before!

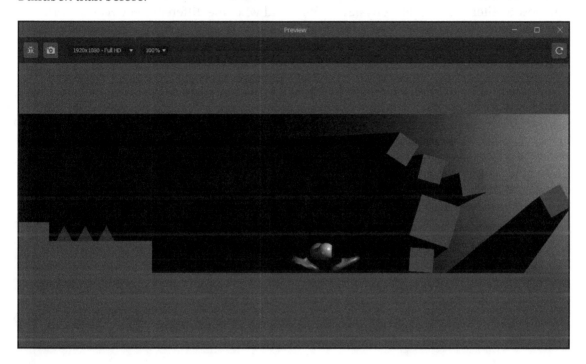

Summary

Ok, so we didn't quite make a complete game. Many of the assets are still just stock template assets. Also, we haven't made any sound. No optimization of assets was done, and we didn't export the game for distribution. Actually, there is a lot more than these subjects that we didn't cover. But this chapter was not about creating a full game.

This chapter was about making you more familiar with Buildbox's interface, methodologies, and processes, which we've done.

You've learned the basics of the Game Mind Map. You now know what nodes are, and how they tie into each other to make a game flow. You also learned how to make navigation buttons, and how those end up making new output channels on nodes. We've also shown you how to alter your world's physics settings, and what the difference between a world and a scene is. And of course, we've learned about how to apply graphics to objects to make your game look great; as well as how to apply collision shapes to your objects. And finally, we learned about instancing, what it is, and how to use it.

Wow…that was a lot for one chapter. But there's a lot more to go as we move into creating a full and complex game using Buildbox. In the next chapter, we begin developing Ramblin' Rover.

Before you begin, if you haven't downloaded the accompanying content as of yet…please do so now. You're going to need it if you'd like to follow the process. Please refer to the *Preface* section of this book for download instructions. Included in the content is a fully compiled version of Ramblin' Rover for both Windows and Mac. You may want to play it, just to see what it is we're going to develop here. You may also download the Ramblin' Rover game for your favorite mobile device from its related app store.

3
Your First Game – Ramblin' Rover, Part 1

Now that you know your way around the Buildbox interface and are familiar with how things are structured in Buildbox, let's dig into the meat of how a game is made. From here on in, we'll be going covering in great detail how we make a game, and the processes, methodologies, and philosophies to follow. Again, if you have not yet downloaded the content (the link is in the *Preface* of this book), please do so now. Let's begin…

Keeping things organized

The most important thing with developing a game is keeping track of your resources. Whether it's in Buildbox (by taking the time to properly name everything) or in your directory structures for assets and naming conventions for those assets, by keeping things organized as you go, you'll greatly minimize your frustration later.

Remember, you may want to update your game later, fix problems, or even make a sequel. Several months or years later, you won't remember that a button was placed in a character folder, or that an asset that should have been named `boulder.png` was named `untitled_object_005` in Buildbox. Naming and organization are key.

Naming conventions

Since we're developing (potentially) for multiple platforms, we have to keep in mind that different platforms handle some file and folder names differently. So, we're going to go old-school with naming conventions. This means we'll be using hump-back notation with no spaces, and we're going to pad any numbers to three spaces. What does this mean? Take a look:

- **Hump-back notation**: This is where the first letter of each word is capitalized and there are no spaces between the words. For example, if you had a star map for a background, the filename would be `StarMap.png`.
- **Padding numbers**: All this means is that if you have more than one image that is similar (or an image sequence for animation), instead of the numbers being 1, 2, 3, they would be 001, 002, 003. For instance, our rover at idle might be `RoverIdle001.png`, `RoverIdle002.png`, and so on.

It's also important to remember to be as descriptive as possible in your naming. Again, you may come back to your project months or even years later. You should make your names so easy to understand that even if you suffer severe head trauma and lose all memory, you'll be able to pick up your project and run with it at a later date.

Directory structure

What good are the most descriptive names on your files if you can't find them? A good directory structure is paramount to good organization. We suggest that you set up your directories before beginning in Buildbox or creating any assets.

How you set up your directories is a matter of personal and professional preference. The following image shows the directory structure we've set up for Ramblin' Rover. The methodology we use for Ramblin' Rover is to simply put every type of asset in its own folder, then, within that folder to put raw files (such as Photoshop PSDs and illustrator AIs in their own folder). Furthermore, any image sequences for animation have their own folders as well:

Since 3D projects have their own plethora of asset files, we simply create a project folder for 3D projects (in Ramblin' Rover's case, we used LightWave, so we have a `Lightwave` folder). But 3D projects are rendered into the respective Buildbox project folders. For example, an animation of a rover's jump; the LightWave project would be kept in the `Lightwave` folder, but the final rendered images would go into `Characters/Rover001-Jump` folder.

As you can see from the previous image, we've followed our naming conventions, kept spaces out of names, and organized our files and folders into something that leads to an environment that is easy to navigate.

We cannot emphasize this enough. Keeping track of your assets will save you a ton of time and frustration.

Creating the game structure

Finally, you're probably saying to yourself right now. Yes, it's been a journey just to start creating our game. But hopefully, all of this prologue has helped you understand that preparation is a key ingredient to a good game. Let's begin with the **Creator** window in Buildbox. Open Buildbox and click the **Create New** button:

The preceding image shows what you should set the creator to. Let's take a look at these settings one by one.

We could get by using all the default settings. But using the **Creator** screen to set up the template will let the software do most of the hard work of creating the game and save a ton of time.

Of course, first we're going to name our game in a simple English way. As this has no bearing on filenames or even the final text for the app, it is just a way to help you later, so we'll use plain English (rather than our naming conventions).

Ramblin' Rover is going to be a driving game, and the direction will go from left to right. Therefore, it's going to be easiest for gameplay if the screen is set to an orientation of **Landscape**. This will help us rotate the screen on the devices and the game itself will look wider compared to a portrait orientation. Also, as most people have their computer displays oriented this way, it will lead to better gameplay on computers and even televisions.

This game will also have leaderboards that are web-enabled so that players can compete with each other on who went furthest. So this game will be endless, and the scoring will be based on distance. So first, let's set the **Score Type** to **Distance**. We'll worry about the endless part soon, but let's cross that bridge later.

The next setting is crucial. In the **Gameplay Settings** area, select **Motocross** from the **Gameplay Type** drop-down menu. This will set up our character as three objects, the main body of our vehicle and two wheels. These wheels will have their own physics so that they will have motors and collisions with the ground while the body of the vehicle will have collisions that will destroy the character if it comes in contact with an obstacle (such as landing on its roof on the ground). We'll go over these connections later so that you know how they work and can recreate them yourself. But for now, why not let the software do as much work for us as possible?

Ramblin' Rover's premise is being able to drive the rover on multiple planets… or really… worlds. So in the **World Settings** pane, let's set the **Game Type** to **Multi World**. Now you should see another set of options pop up in this area. Here is where we can set up the general settings for our worlds. Let's set the **World Amount** to **3**. Of course, this makes our game have three worlds. Each world is another game in itself, with its own rules for physics, its own backgrounds, and even, unique scales for character.

Remember how we said our game would be endless? An endless game is one where there simply is no end to the level. Generally, they get progressively harder but can be games where they're filled with difficult obstacles that repeat in random orders, giving the player a repetitive but unique experience as the game progresses. I know, those two things are diametrically opposed. However, if you think of it like a bag of trail mix it may be easier to understand. Trail mix is filled with peanuts, raisins, and chocolate. Think of each obstacle as one of these items. When you eat this trail mix in general, the order you get pieces is random. While eating, you get different flavors depending on that order. Similarly, while playing an endless game, you get a different experience by changing up the order of the obstacles.

Endless games are also more resource-efficient. The player can play a longer game without the need for more scenes in the game. Typically, an endless game can be anywhere from 5-15 scenes per world, where a goal-oriented game (completing a level) may have many more. Both types of game are definitely worthwhile. However, as we're having three worlds and our limitation on mobile is 100 MB, we need to stay as light on resources as possible. Let's make sure our **World End Action** is set to `Endless`.

Let's also make sure that the checkbox for **Single UI for World** is *ticked*. This will make it so that our controls, sensors, and score indicators are the same across all worlds. Again, this will make things a bit lighter. Since our worlds will never end, leave the **World Complete UI** *unticked*.

Finally, let's tick every checkbox in the **Menu Settings**. This will create menu UIs so we can have Informational, Pause, Game Over, and Coin Shop screens within the game.

Alrighty, let's move on. Once you click on the **Create** button, you'll go to the first world of your game. It should look like the following screenshot:

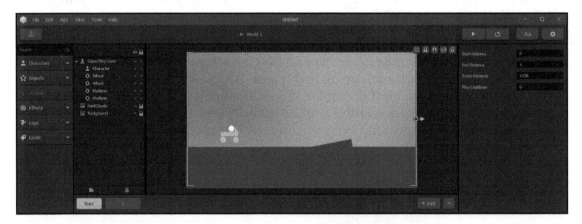

This is the initial template for our game set with characters, pre-defined physics and even some obstacles. All are set on the stage as primitives for us to replace and adjust

Cool, right? We now have a full template for our Ramblin' Rover game. Now, we just need to do some tweaks, add some menus and music, and set up our physics. Before we dive too deep into our new game, let's take a look at the Game Mind Map that our **Create** menu settings have made.

The initial Game Mind Map

Start off by clicking the **Game Mind Map** button (top left). As you can see, this is a much more intricate map than we saw with our last tutorial. Your Game Mind Map should look like the following screenshot:

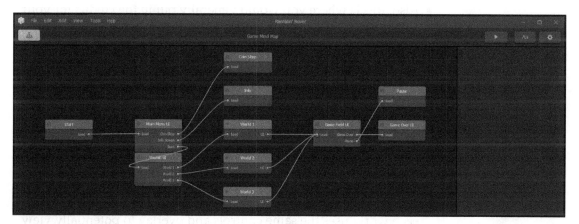

As before, the green boxes are UIs (which can be either UI overlays for worlds, or menus) and the blue boxes are our game worlds. Let's break down our user experience flow from left to right:

- Let's start with the node labelled **Start**:
    - This is also known as a Loading Splash Screen.
    - We can put our game or company logo, and a loading status bar.
    - This screen is only shown while the rest of the game buffers into memory. (Buffering into memory is a fancy way of saying that the game is loading into usable memory space, and once it's finished, it can be played.)

- Once the game is loaded, the user is taken to the **Main Menu** UI node. From here, the user can choose the following options:
  - Play the game.
  - Get info from the informational screen.
  - Visit the coin shop to gain coins (for real-world money) to unlock items within our game. Of course, we'll set up coins in our game that players can earn, but why capitalize from people that want shortcuts?
- **Info** screens are just that…informational:
  - Instructions on how to play the game.
  - Information about the storyline.
  - Even links to developer web pages and other games you may have developed.
  - Also, this is where you would generally put in the credits for your game assets. If you've played Ramblin' Rover (the final version), you may have seen this screen with several TurboSquid and public domain credits. These are generally required under the license if you use third-party objects and assets.
- Next is the **Worlds UI** screen:
  - The player will be able to select which world they will play in. In the Ramblin' Rover game, this will be where players will select the planet they can drive the rover on.
  - From the **Worlds UI**, you can see that it splits off to three distinct worlds. But you may also notice that each world splits off and comes back together on the **Game Field UI**. All this means is that each world uses the same controls and overlay to potentially view your score. They also then go off to the **Game Over UI** and the **Pause** screen.

And there you have it. Our entire (current) game flow. Want a preview of how things will look when we're done? Well, by the time we're done with this game, it will look like the following screenshot, and you will understand *everything*:

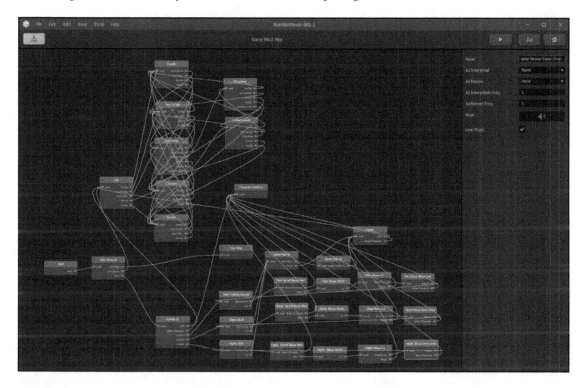

Crazy, right? Well, don't worry. We're going to build this step by step, and this will eventually look very simple to you.

For now, let's move on.

Placeholder objects and initial stage setup

Let's dive back into our stage and start replacing our placeholder objects. Start by double-clicking on the **World 1** node. So now we're back to seeing our stage for **World 1**. If you hover your mouse over the character (the little yellow truck with a ball on it), you can use your mouse wheel to zoom in. Click on the **Activate Connection Mode** button at the top-right of the stage, and zoom in so that Buildbox looks like the following screenshot:

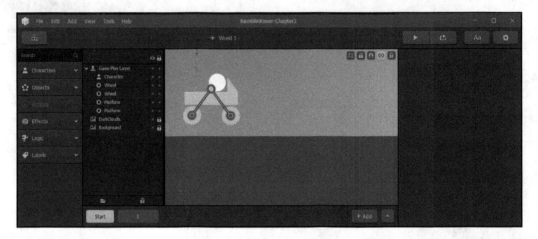

Connections and parenting (the basics)

Connections can be used for multiple purposes. The image above shows that the wheels are connected to the car. Unlike our other basic platformer game, a motocross game uses the wheels to propel the character across the ground (rather than the character directly moving).

When you've activated your connection mode, each object appears to have an orange circle in the center of it. This is the connection point. Connections are always drawn by dragging from one orange circle to the next. The order is pretty simple…always draw from the parent to the child. In this case, if the connections weren't already drawn, we would go from the character to the wheel. The child's orange circle then turns red to indicate that it is a child.

So, that's how the car drives. The wheels have controls assigned to them to make them motors, and because the wheels (our actual character) are attached to the body, it moves with them, just like a real car.

We'll be using connections in a more advanced way in a later chapter, but for now, let's make this game look better.

Stage borders (the game frame)

Turn on the **Show Game Frame** button (top right of the stage). The game frame is basically the area where your character is restricted to, and how it is restricted. You should see a box appear on the left side of the visible stage. It currently has all-gray borders. This means that the character can travel up, down, left, and right and the game will scroll to keep the character within that box. We want to set up some restrictions on that border.

By clicking on any of the gray lines that make up the box, we change that line to orange. What this means is that the character cannot travel beyond that point. Do this to the top line of the game-frame. Now, our character can't jump off the area we're creating.

Next, click twice on the line that makes up the bottom of the box. You'll see that line turn red. This means that if the character touches this line, the character will be destroyed. Now, we can set up pits that if the character falls into them, the character explodes and dies.

Finally, on the corners of the box, you'll see little orange circles. These are handles that let you change the shape of the box. Using one of these handles on the left side of the box, let's move the left side in a bit so that if the rover backs up, the screen begins to scroll before the character reaches the edge. The results will look like the following screenshot:

Preparing graphic assets for use in Buildbox

Ok, so as we said before, the only graphic assets that Buildbox can use are PNG files. If this was just a simple tutorial on how to make Ramblin' Rover we could leave it there. But it's not. Ramblin' Rover is just an example of how a game is made, but we want to give you all of the tools and base-knowledge you need to create all of your own games from scratch. Even if you don't create your own graphic assets, you need to be able to tell anybody creating them for you how you want them…and more importantly, you need to know why.

Graphics are absolutely the most important thing in developing a game. After all, you saw how just some eyes and sneakers made a cute character people want to see move in the previous chapter. Graphics create your world. They create characters that people want to succeed. Most importantly, graphics create the feel of your game, and differentiate it from other games on the market.

What exactly is a PNG file?

Anybody remember GIF files? No, not animated GIFs that you see in most chat-rooms and on Facebook (although they are related). Back in the 1990s, a still-frame GIF file was the best way to have a graphics file that had a transparent background. GIFs can be used for animation, and can have a number of different purposes. However, GIFs were clunky. How so? Well, they had a type of compression known as lossy. This just means that when compressed, information was lost, and artifacts and noise could pop up and be present.

Furthermore, GIFs used indexed colors. This means that anywhere from two colors to 256 could be used, and that's why you see something known as banding in GIF imagery.

Banding is where something in real life goes from dark to light because of lighting and shadows. In real life, it's a smooth transition known as a gradient. With indexed colors, banding can occur when these various shades are outside of the index. In this case, the colors of these pixels are quantized (or snapped) to the nearest color in the index. The images below show a noisy and banded GIF (left) vs the original picture (right):

So, along came **Portable Network Graphics** (**PNGs**). Originally, the PNG format was what a program called **Macromedia Fireworks** used to save projects. Now, that same software is called Adobe Fireworks and is part of the Creative Cloud. Fireworks would cut up a graphics file into a table or image map and make areas of the image clickable via hyperlink for HTML web files. PNGs were still not widely supported by web browsers, so it would export the final web files as GIFs or JPEGs.

But somewhere along the line, someone realized that the PNG image itself was extremely bandwidth-efficient. So, in the 2000s, PNGs started to see some support on browsers. Up until around 2008, though, Microsoft's Internet Explorer still did not support PNGs with transparency, so some strange CSS hacks needed to be done to utilize them.

Today, though, the PNG file is the most widely used network-based image file. It's lossless, has great transparency, and is extremely efficient. Since PNGs are so widely used, this is probably why Buildbox restricts compatibility to that format. Remember, Buildbox can export for multiple mobile and desktop platforms.

Alright, so PNGs are great and very compatible. But there are multiple flavors of PNG files. So, what differentiates them?

What bit-ratings mean

When dealing with bit-ratings, you have to understand that when you hear *8-bit image* and *24-bit image* that it may be talking about two different types of rating, or even exactly the same type of image. Confused? Good, because when dealing with a graphics professional to create your assets, you're going to have to be a lot more specific, so let's give you a brief education in this.

Your typical image is 8 bits per channel (8 bpc), or 24 bits total (because there are three channels: red, green, and blue). This is also what they mean by a 16.7 million-color image. The math is pretty simple. A bit is either 0 or 1. 8 bits may look something like 01100110. That means that there are 256 possible combinations on that channel. Why? Because to calculate the number of possibilities, you take the number of possible values per slot and take it to that power. 0 or *1*... that's 2 possibilities and 8-bit is 8 slots. *2 x 2 x 2 x 2 x 2 x 2 x 2 x 2* (2 to the 8th power) is 256. To combine colors on a pixel, you'd need to multiply the possibilities such as 256 x 256 x 256 (which is 16.7 million). That's how they know that there are 16.7 million possible colors in an 8 bpc or 24-bit image. So saying 8 bit may mean per channel, or overall. That's why it's extremely important to add the word *channel* if that's what you mean.

Finally, there is a fourth channel, called **alpha**. The alpha channel is the transparency channel. So when you're talking about a 24-bit PNG with transparency, you're really talking about a 32-bit image. Why is this important to know? Because some graphics programs (such as Photoshop) have 24-bit PNG as an option with a checkbox for transparency. But some other programs (such as the 3D software we used called *LightWave*) have an option for a 24-bit PNG and a 32-bit PNG. These are essentially the same as the Photoshop options, but with different names. By understanding what these bits per channel are, and what they do, you can navigate your image-creating software options better.

So, what's an 8-bit PNG, and why is it so important to differentiate it from an 8-bit per channel PNG (or 24-bit PNG)? Because an 8-bit PNG is highly compressed. Much like a GIF, it uses indexed colors. It also uses a great algorithm to *dither* or blend the colors to fill them in to avoid banding. 8-bit PNG files are *extremely* efficient on resources (that is, they are much smaller files), but still look good, unless they have transparency.

Because they are so highly compressed, the alpha channel is included in that 8-bits. So, if you use 8-bit PNG files for objects that require transparency, they will end up with a white-ghosting effect around them, and look terrible on screen, much like a weather report where the weather reporter's green screen is bad.

So, the rule is...

So, what all this means to you is pretty simple. For objects that require transparency channels, always use 24-bit PNG files with transparency (also called 8 bits per channel, or 32-bit images). For objects that have no transparency (such as block-shaped obstacles and objects), use 8-bit PNG files. By following this rule, you'll keep your game looking great while avoiding *bloating* your project files. In the end, Buildbox repacks all of the images in your project into atlases (which we'll cover later) that are 32 bit. However, it's always a good practice to stay lean.

If you were a Buildbox 1.x user, you may remember that Buildbox had some issues with DPI (dots per inch) between the standard 72 and 144 on retina displays. This issue is a thing of the past with Buildbox 2.

Image sequences

We dealt with them in the last chapter briefly, but what are they really? Think of a film strip. It's just a sequence of still-images known as frames. Your standard United States film runs at 24 frames per second (well, really 23.976, but let's just round up for our purposes). Also, in the US, television runs at 30 frames per second (again, 29.97, but whatever... let's round up).

Remember that each image in our sequence is a full image with all of the resources associated with it. We can quite literally cut our necessary resources in half by cutting this to 15 frames per second (fps).

If you open the content you downloaded, and navigate to `Projects/RamblinRover/Characters/Rover001-Body`, you'll see that the images are named `Rover001-body_001.png`, `Rover001-body_002.png`, and so on. The final number indicates the number that should play in the sequence (first `001`, then `002`, and so on).

The animation is really just the satellite dish rotating, and the scanner light in the window rotating as well. But what you'll really notice is that this animation is loopable.

All loopable means is that the animation can loop (play over and over again) without you noticing a bump in the footage (the final frame leads seamlessly back to the first).

If you're not creating these animations yourself, you'll need to make sure to specify to your graphics professional to make these animations loopable at 15 fps. They should understand exactly what you mean, and if they don't...you may consider finding a new animator.

Recommended software for graphics assets

We really covered this in the first chapter. However, for the purposes of context (now that you understand more about graphics and Buildbox), a bit of reinforcement couldn't hurt.

A key piece of graphics software is the Adobe Creative Cloud subscription (`http://www.ad obe.com/creativecloud.html`). Given its *bang for the buck*, it just can't be beat. With it, you'll get Photoshop (which can be used for all graphics assets from your game's icon to obstacles and other objects), Illustrator (which is great for navigational buttons), After Effects (very useful for animated image sequences), Premiere Pro (a video editing application for marketing videos from screen-captured gameplay), and Audition (for editing all your sound).

You may also want some 3D software, such as LightWave, 3D Studio Max, or Maya. This can greatly improve the ability to make characters, enemies, and to create still renders for menus and backgrounds. Most of the assets in Ramblin' Rover were created with the 3D software LightWave.

Of course, as mentioned in `Chapter 1`, *So, You Want to Develop a Video Game?*, there are free options for all of these tools. However, there are not nearly as many tutorials and resources available on the web to help you learn and create using these.

One key thing to remember when using free software: if it's free…you're the product. In other words, some benefits come with paid software, such as better support, and being part of the industry standard. Free software seems to be in a perpetual state of *beta testing*.

If using free software, read your **End User License Agreement** (**EULA**) very carefully. Some software may require you to credit them in some way for the privilege of using their software for profit. They may even lay claim to part of your profits.

Ok, let's get to actually using our graphics in Ramblin' Rover…

Setting up our rover

The following screenshot shows how images are currently set up with our character (left) and where they will be soon (right):

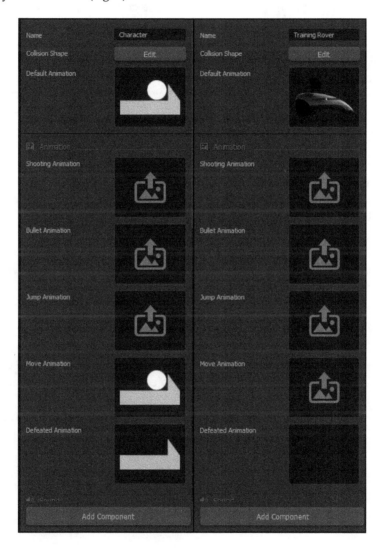

We'll do this the same way we did in the last chapter, Chapter 2, *Orientation*:

- In the **Asset Library**, open the **Characters** section and select the **Character**.
- Rename the character **Training Rover** in the **Properties** window. You may think this violates our naming conventions. Those conventions are for files, not for elements in our Buildbox game. It's important to name your objects in plain English. That way, when it comes to choosing characters or unlocking new ones, they are readable in our store.
- Now open your file browser to our content directory and navigate to Projects/RamblinRover/Characters/Rover001-Body; select all of the images in that folder and drag them to the **Default Animation** field.
- If you hover your mouse over the **Move Animation** field, you'll see two options in the upper-right of the field. One looks like a pencil, and this is the **Edit** button. The other looks like an **X**; this is the **Remove** button. Click on the **Remove** button so there is no longer a **Move Animation**. We do this because the wheels will do the actual moving, not the character. A **Move Animation** is superfluous, and we want to remain resource efficient.
- Finally, navigate your file browser window to Projects/RamblinRover/Explosions/boom001. Then, select all the images in this folder and drag them to the Defeated Animation field. This will make the character explode when it is destroyed.

We'll eventually do a lot more with this character in a later section. But for now, the basic body of our rover is complete. Let's move on to the wheels.

The image below shows the wheels already replaced. This is done the same way as the character. In the **Asset Library**, select the **Wheel** object from the **Objects** section. Drag the Rover001-Wheel.png image from your file browser (located in Projects/RamblinRover/Characters) to the **Default Animation** field in the properties window. Well, things definitely look a little jacked up, don't they? We'll fix this momentarily:

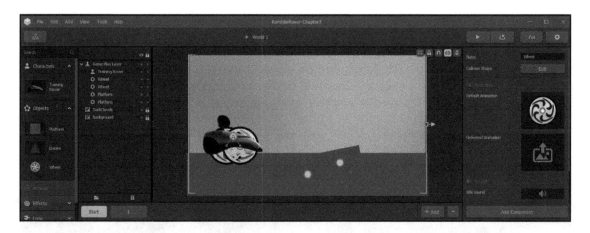

The reason why our character went a little wonky is because the resolution of our new images is higher than the resolution of the old placeholders. Also, the wheels appear behind our rover, so let's fix that problem first. In the **Layers** window, simply drag the **Training Rover** under both Wheel objects. When complete, your **Layers** window should look like the following screenshot:

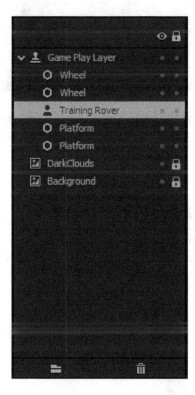

Now we need to scale and position the objects so that our rover looks proper.

First, select the body of the Rover. This can be done in either the **Layer** window or by clicking on the body on the Stage. Sometimes, objects can overlap, and selecting on the Stage can be difficult. The **Layer** window makes this a bit easier. Set both the **Scale** fields to 0.35. Now the body of the rover is a more playable size.

Next, we need to scale the wheels. Select each wheel, and set their **Scale** fields to 0.18. Now that this is done, you can just drag the wheels so that their positions line up properly with the rover. We've zoomed in so you can see the rover better. It should look like the following screenshot:

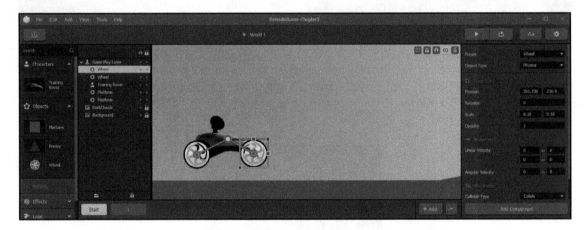

Awesome! So our Rover looks great now, but it won't work right just yet. That's because the collision shapes are not set up yet. We'll get to that in a moment. First, though, let's set up our backgrounds.

Creating our backgrounds

Let's zoom out so we can see the entire stage. After all, if we're editing something that affects the entire stage, we should probably see what we're working with. We should also remove all the obstacles and background objects in the scene.

In the Layer window, let's select each of the **Platform** objects and hit the *Delete* key on your keyboard. You might notice that both the **DarkClouds** and **Background** layers are locked. To unlock them, just click the little padlock icon on their layer. There is also a global background lock/unlock button (in the top-right corner of the viewport). It can make for an easy shortcut to lock, or unlock all of the background layers. Now you can select each of these layers and delete them the same way as the **Platform** objects. The result should look like this:

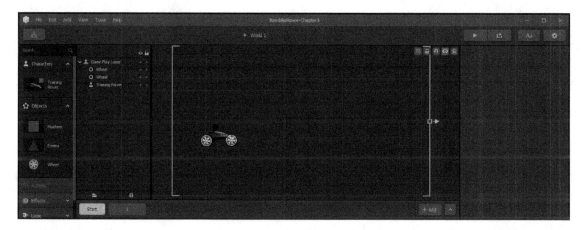

The reason we did this is that we're going to fully replace the background with several layers that will move in parallax. Parallax is a fancy way of describing an aspect of perspective. This movement gives the illusion that our character is moving through a three-dimensional world (even though it's not). You can demonstrate parallax to yourself pretty easily. Hold both of your hands up in front of your face, one in front of the other with about 6 inches of separation. Now, move them (together) back and forth (from left to right, then right to left). You'll see that across your visual area, the hand at the back crosses behind the hand at the front. That's parallax. How do we accomplish this? Let's place our backgrounds, and then you'll see how we can do this using movement parameters.

Start by navigating your file browser to `Projects/RamblinRover/Backgrounds`. Drag the `MarsGradient.png` to your stage, but *DO NOT RELEASE* your mouse button. You should see an overlay pop up over the stage that looks like the following screenshot. You can now release your mouse button over the **Background** section of this overlay (at the bottom right):

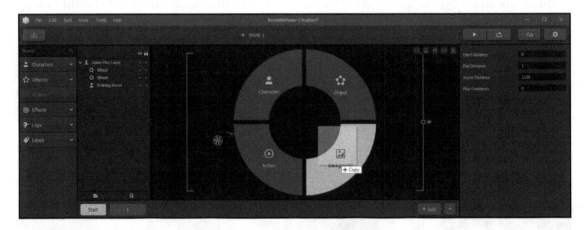

You should see the whole stage turn rather orange. Don't worry, this is normal. It's because all new objects appear at the top of the Layers. Just drag the `MarsGradient` object in the **Layers** window to the bottom, as you can see in the following screenshot:

Ok, so what we've just done is create the Martian sky. Just in case you haven't guessed by now, our first world will be on Mars. If you open the `MarsGradient.png` file in an image editing program, you'll notice that it's tall and very thin. The reason for this is that backgrounds are tiled horizontally. This means that the image is simply repeated infinitely from left to right. Since our image is just a gradient going from pink at the top to orange at the bottom, we didn't need to make it very wide. This helps us stay lean on resources. You should be constantly thinking of ways to cut down on your resource usage as you make your games.

Ok, let's add another background element. Follow the same steps to bring in
`SunFlareGlow.png` as a background layer. Put this layer just above the `MarsGradient`
layer in the layer window. As you walk, or drive your car, what's the one piece of scenery
that never moves? The Sun. So, we need to set the **Speed** parameter in the properties
window to 0. Let's also set this graphic up so that it's positioned properly.

This graphic is one of only a few that is not seamless for the background. A seamless image
is one that (when repeated) blends smoothly. You cannot see a seam in a seamless image.
As the **SunFlareGlow** background is not seamless, we need to position it so that users do
not see any seams.

We've already set it so that it never moves while the rover is driving. Let's set the **Position**
attributes in the **Properties** window to 0.1 and 320 respectively. Now set the **Scale**
attributes to 0.75 and 0.84 respectively. We know, it looks a little jacked up (in that we can
see a clear seam) on our stage. The problem is not how our stage looks, it's how our
playable game looks, and in that respect, the problem is solved. You'll see what we mean
when we test the game.

We arrived at these numbers by opening the preview screen over and over again, and
tweaking these numbers until the image was positioned properly. Your result should look
like this:

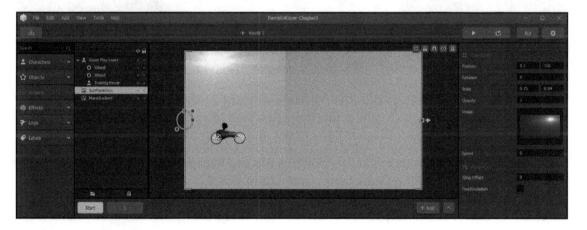

To add some realism to our game, we're going to add some lens reflections as well. The sun shows up on a camera as a lens flare. There are several elements to a lens flare, but two major ones: the actual glow (which we've just placed) and lens reflections. Lens reflections show up as geometric shapes as light reflects off the layers of glass inside a lens. Since this light is reflecting inside the lens, these reflections show up on top of any other image the camera sees. This is why it's a separate image; so we can put this layer on top of everything else.

Drag the `SunFlareReflections.png` file onto the stage as a Background. This time, we'll leave this at the top of our Layer window. Set all of the parameters of this layer to the exact same values as our **SunFlareGlow** layer. The result should look like the following screenshot:

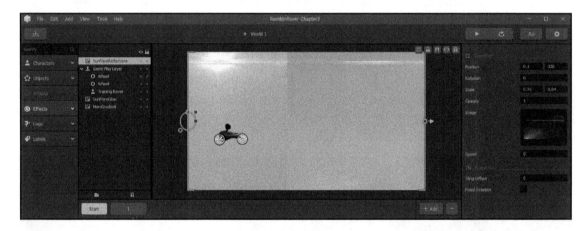

Granted, it doesn't look all *that* different. But this will add a nice effect that will give the game field a bit of extra polish. We've taken the first step toward parallax as well. We've identified a far-distant object (the Sun) that never moves. Now, let's build that forward.

Go ahead and bring in the `MartianClouds.png` file as a Background. We'll move this layer down just above the SunFlareGlow layer. Its **Position** should be set to 0.1 by 320. We'll leave the scale alone. This image *is* seamless, and will move across the sky slowly as our rover drives. So, we'll set its **Speed** parameter to 0.15. The result should look like this:

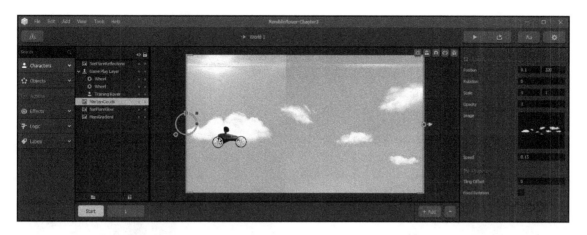

Now let's add some mountains. Bring in the `DistanceMountains.png` file just above the **MartianClouds** layer as (you guessed it) another Background. Set this layer's **Position** to `0.1` by `135`, and let's scale it down a bit. Please set the **Scale** to `0.772` by `0.688`. The mountains are still pretty distant, but much closer than the clouds. So their **Speed** will be `0.35`.

Seeming tedious yet? With all of these parameters, scales, and positions, you may feel a bit lost in the numbers. Don't worry, we'll do one more background layer and then we'll explain everything that just happened. At this point, your screen should look like the following screenshot:

Now, we'll throw in our Martian landscape. This image was taken from the actual Mars Rover, and is really the surface of Mars! NASA is a great resource for images. They are a government agency, and thus all the images that NASA produces are considered public domain. What this means is that you're free to use them in any way you wish. It's just advisable to give these images a credit on your info screens.

Go ahead and bring the `MarsLand.png` file in as a background and place it just above the **DistanceMountains** layer. Set the **Position** to 0.1 by 107 and the **Scale** to 0.49 by 0.582. Finally, since this is our mid-ground layer, let's set its **Speed** to 0.5. And, as always, your result should resemble the following screenshot:

A summary of backgrounds and parallax

Just in case you felt a bit lost with everything we just did, it's probably best to give it a brief once-over…or really a twice-over. Using rates of speed, we can create the illusion of parallax. The **Speed** parameter of a background lets you set how fast it scrolls by as you move. By setting the farthest object (the Sun) to 0 **Speed**, we've made it hold position no matter where our rover may go.

By setting the **Speed** value progressively higher with each object closer to our foreground, we can make them move by at faster rates. This is the essence of the illusion of Parallax. The one exception to this rule is the Sun **FlareReflections** layer. But since this is really just an additional part of the Sun, its Speed is the same as the Sun **FlareGlow** layer (which is 0).

We've also positioned all of our backgrounds in the proper places (clouds in the sky, mountains peaking over our landscape, and the Mars landscape at the bottom of the screen.)

Let's make sure we don't inadvertently change the background that we worked so hard to place. Let's lock each layer we just worked on by clicking the little gray dot on the far right of each layer in the **Layer** window (the dot falling under the padlock icon at the top of the **Layer** window). You should now have a **Layer** window that looks like the following screenshot:

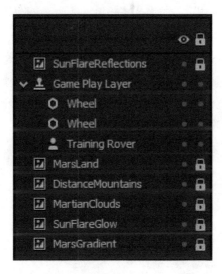

Collisions and obstacles

We can't wait for you to see your parallax backgrounds, but right now the game is not testable. There is no ground to drive on, and our rover still needs its collision shapes adjusted. If you remember from our previous chapter, collision shapes must be edited in the base object, and not the instance on the game stage. So, let's start with the wheels.

In the asset library, open the **Objects** section and select the **Wheel**. In the properties window, you'll see a field called **CollisionShape**. Click the **Edit** button for this field.

Within the shape editor, you can see that the current collision shape barely covers the axle of the wheel. Let's expand this selection using the handle (a small dot) on the right side of the circle to cover the entire wheel. It should look like the following screenshot:

Since we did this with the master object for the wheels (and not the two instances of the wheels on our stage), both wheels are affected by this new shape. Now the wheels will actually roll on the ground, rather than falling through it.

Now let's take care of the rover's collision shape. Following the same process as we did in Chapter 2, *Orientation*, let's adjust the polygon shape of the rover's body by adding points and dragging them around until the shape looks like the following screenshot:

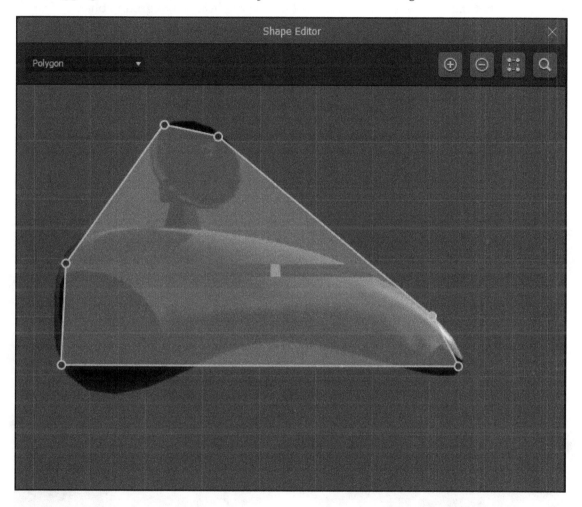

Great, now our rover is set up (basically) to drive. We just need something to drive on!

 Remember, if the polygon turns red, it's not usable in Buildbox. So, shapes cannot have any concave angles. Every angle must be convex.

Placing the ground

In a motocross game, the ground and obstacles are somewhat synonymous. The ground is an obstacle that can destroy our character, but not every obstacle is a ground object. We add obstacle objects the same way we added backgrounds with one exception. In the `Projects/RamblinRover/Ground` folder, you'll find `GroundBlockCutaway-Mars.png`. Drag that file over the stage, and let it go over the **Objects** part of the overlay that pops up as illustrated in the following screenshot:

Now we just need to position our first ground-block and set up its actions. Drag the **GroundBlockCutaway** object that's on the stage down to the bottom left so that it's a little below the visible area. It should look like this:

What we're doing here is creating a base instance of the ground block. Once we get all of the settings correct, we'll duplicate this across the visible area of the stage. In the properties window, scroll down to the bottom. You'll see a **Properties** section in the properties window. This is where we can set collision actions.

Collisions and collision actions

A collision is exactly what it sounds like: something that will happen when two objects' collision shapes intersect. By default, when a new object is put on the stage, its **Collision Type** is set to **Collide**. All this means is that this parameter is telling the program that "yes, we'd like this object to make something happen when another object touches it."

In the next chapter (Chapter 4, *Advanced World Design —Ramblin' Rover, Part 2*), we'll have some objects that have a **No Collide** setting. That setting is for what we call *decorations*, for example, a tree that you don't want to be a background element (because background elements are tiled). Then, you can drive right by a tree without anything happening, and you can place that tree wherever you'd like on the level without it automatically tiling across your whole world.

 Remember… every stage on your world shares the same background.

The next parameter is **Destroy Type**. By default, this is set to **No Destroy**. Set this to **Destroy Character** so that it looks like the image on the right.

Let's take a quick look at what each setting in this parameter does:

- **No Destroy:** Two different things can happen when an object comes in contact with this. First, if this is not a physics object, then it will not let anything pass. It's a brick wall. Your character will stop dead, or bounce off it. Second, if it is a physics object, it will bounce off your character, get pushed by it, or react in some other way, but nothing will be destroyed…only interact with it based on physics parameters.

- **Destroy Character:** If your character touches this object, your character will be destroyed, and the game will be over.
- **Destroy Enemy:** This is where you might use the object as something to throw or push at an enemy to destroy it. Think of it as the shell of a turtle in *Super Mario Bros.* Jump on it once, and it destroys the actual turtle head and legs (beneath), then on the bounce it shoots across the screen, you can run behind it, and it destroys your enemies.
- **Destroy All:** This is bad… really bad for anything that touches it. It will literally destroy anything and everything that comes in contact with it.

Creating more instances

Now, we're set with the ground-block template. Creating more instances that look just like this is pretty easy. Just press the *D* key on your keyboard, and another instance is created to the right. Press this key four more times and the ground stretches out across the visible area.

On the right of the visible area, you'll see a large orange bracket with a small orange rectangle in the center. You'll also see a small orange arrow just to the right of that square. Drag this little orange square to the right until the bracket goes to the edge of the last ground-block. This extends the scene so that it holds all of the ground-blocks. Your final Start scene should look like the following screenshot:

Before we move on, let's clean up some resources. As we're not going to be using any of our original obstacles, let's eliminate them from our asset library. In the **Objects** section of our library, select and delete (by clicking on the little **X** on the top-right of their icons) the **Platform** and **Enemy** objects.

Now, let's create our first obstacle on Scene 1!

Working with scenes

Before we switch to Scene 1, let's highlight the **GroundBlockCutaway-Mars** object on the far left by clicking on it. Now, load it into your computer's clipboard by copying it (*Ctrl + C* in Windows or *Cmd + C* on Mac). Why did we copy this one into memory? Because not only are we now able to copy the object to another scene, but its exact position. Since we're rolling from one scene to the next, we'll want to have the height of the first block of our next scene be the same height as the last block of this scene. And, since all of the blocks are the same height in the Start scene, why not copy the first block? Then its left-to-right position is also set and we won't have to move it.

Now, in the scene selection window (at the bottom of Buildbox), click on the button with a number **1** on it. You'll see an empty scene with our backgrounds in it, and a ghost image of our rover. Paste the **GroundBlockCutaway-Mars** object onto the stage by using *Ctrl + V* in Windows, or *Cmd + V* on Mac. The result should look like this:

First, let's get a good ground layer to cover a fairly decent sized scene. With the **GroundBlockCutaway-Mars** selected on the stage, hit the D key on your keyboard 10 times. This will create 10 instances of the ground-block that go well beyond the end of the visible scene. As we did before, grab that bracket-handle (the little square on the right bracket) and extend the scene to the end of the ground-blocks. You'll need to zoom out (using the mouse wheel) to see the whole scene now.

Now, let's create a jump-ramp. Select the fifth block from the left. All of those little squares that line the edge of the selection box are for scaling. The round one in the bottom-left corner is for rotating the block. First, we're going to make the block taller. Drag the vertical-scale handle (the one in the center of the top of the selection square) up until the scale is around 1.4. Now, use that rotational handle (the circle at the bottom-left of the selection square) to rotate the block to somewhere between -13 and -14 degrees. Then, you can position the block so that there are no gaps visually between this block and the previous block, and line up the left corner to the top of the previous block.

Follow the same procedure to make another section of the ramp that's steeper. Select the sixth block from the left, and set the vertical scale to somewhere around 2.25 and the rotation to around -31.5 degrees. Then delete the seventh block by selecting it and hitting the *Delete* key on your keyboard. This will create a gap to force drivers to keep their momentum up, and not simply drive over the ramp, but to take it at speed and jump the gap. And these are the results:

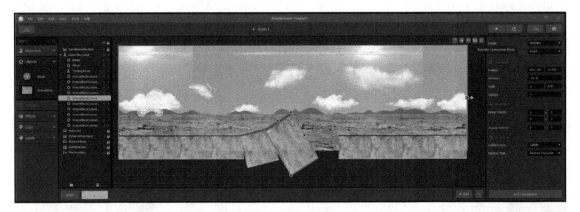

Neat, so we have a jump. But let's take it a step further. The bonus to an endless game is that by combining the different obstacles, the way they approach each one will vary by the previous obstacle's exit. So, let's ensure that this obstacle isn't a gimme if they're going too slow. Let's raise the exit blocks a bit.

Let's begin with the fourth block from the right. Vertically scale it to around 1.9, and move it up so that the top is about even with the top of the ramp. Then, on the third block from the right, let's scale that to around 1.5 and move it up to split the difference in height between the fourth and second from the right to create stair steps. The results should look like this:

I know, you're probably itching to test all of this out. Well, let's get the controls together so that the game is playable, and then we can!

Setting up testing controls

Since we're testing this on a computer, what we really need is to set up the keyboard as a controller. By default, the controls make little sense, and some controls are assigned that don't need to be. Let's open up our controller settings and fix all this…

At the top right of Buildbox, you'll notice an icon that looks like a gear. It's the **Settings** button, and you should click it.

You're now in the **General** settings screen. We'll come back to this in a later chapter when we talk about exporting the game for platforms. For now, what we want is the **Controllers** settings screen, so click the **Controllers** button at the top of the window. You'll be confronted with the following interface:

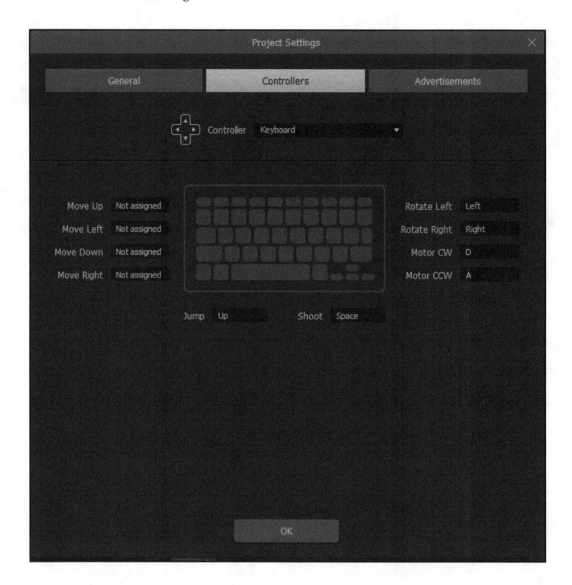

To set up which key does what function, just click in the field, and hit the key. We removed the settings on the move controls by just clicking in the field and hitting the backspace key on our keyboard. Set up the keys in the following way:

- **Rotate left**: Left arrow
- **Rotate right**: Right arrow
- **Motor CW**: *D*
- **Motor CCW**: *A*
- **Jump**: Up arrow
- **Shoot**: Space bar

Ok, so this is what all of these settings do: The Motor controls control the wheels' torque direction (which direction they spin). CW means clockwise, and CCW means counter clockwise (same as anti-clockwise for you UK folks). This means that *A* on your keyboard will be reverse, and *D* will be forward. Essentially, we'll be using the *W*, *A*, *S* and *D* keys that gamers are used to in order to control the direction of the rover itself.

The **Rotate** directions have nothing to do with the wheels. This puts a small rotational force on the character itself. It's how a motorcyclist would pop a wheelie, and can be used to help influence flips when in the air.

Our rover will be using jump jets (eventually), so we'll use the up arrow (since a player will already have their right hand ready on the arrow keys) to give that jump a jet boost; once we set up the jump capabilities.

Testing and adjusting physics

Let's go ahead and test the game for the first time. We haven't set up all the physics yet, but let's just see where we're at. Once you click on the **Preview** button (at the top-right of Buildbox), you'll see this screen:

Remember how we have the Game Mind Map laid out? This is the current state of our Main Menu UI. Click on **Start**, and you'll be taken to the screen below and left (the **Worlds UI**), and finally, when you click on **1** (for world number 1), you'll be taken to Mars and can play (the screen to the lower-right). Play with it, and then we'll move on.

Making the game easier to test

Until we get to making our UI screens look better, we don't want to have to go through all of these menus every time we make a tiny adjustment. So, let's adjust our Game Mind Map so that when we hit our Preview button, it takes us straight to the area we're testing. Go ahead and open the Game Mind Map.

What we need is to literally skip-over our **Menu UI** and **Worlds UI** and go straight to **World 1**. So, grab the handle on the Load output of our Start node, and drag it straight to the **Load** input of the **World 1** node. The results are depicted in the following screenshot:

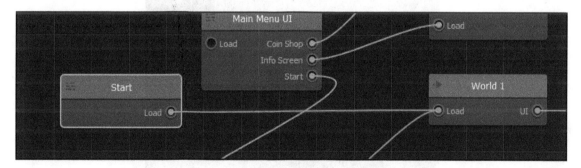

Now if we test our game, we'll go straight to the game (instead of the menus). Go ahead and try it out!

Adjusting the physics

Ok, so our current game is slow and boring. But we don't want it to be too hard. As Mars is only the first world, it must be attainable, yet moderately challenging. Single-click on the **World 1** node, and let's edit its properties. Rename this world **Mars Training Ground**, and set all of the properties to match the following image. Let's go through these settings…

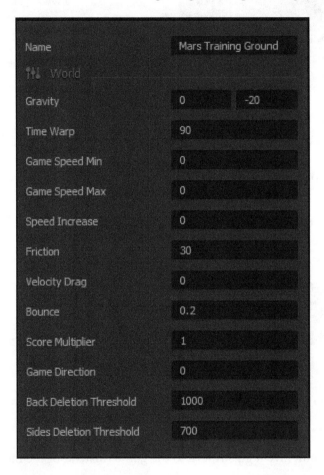

Mars is a little less than half the size of the Earth, so the rover needs to seem to float through the air a bit. So let's reduce the vertical gravity by changing it to -20. We do want to make sure the rover can go somewhat fast, so bringing up the **Time Warp** to 90 will help with this. Also, Mars is a very dusty environment, so we want the rover to *peel out* as it accelerates. So, we'll reduce our friction to 30. Finally, because of the reduced gravity, we'll also want the rover to bounce a bit when it hits the ground, but not so much that it's uncontrollable. Ergo, we'll raise the **Bounce** parameter to 0.2.

We're not done yet with adjusting our physics settings, but go ahead and test it out now just to see what our new settings for the world have done.

Ok! So now that we've set up the physics for our world, let's set them up for the rover. Go ahead and open the World 1 node, which is now the **Mars Training Ground** node. Once we're in our world, let's open the **Training Rover** character's properties from the asset library. You'll need to scroll down to the **Character Gameplay Settings** in the property window, and adjust them so that they resemble the following image. Again, let's go through these one at a time.

First off, even with the **Time Warp** setting we did on the world, the rover is just not fast enough to feel very fun. So we can increase the horizontal max speed to 90. We're going to leave the rest of the settings alone for now, and just change both the **Left Lean Force** and **Right Lean Force** to 60. We'll revisit this area when we set up jumping later. But for now, we don't need the character itself to bounce (as we don't need the body to bounce…it just blows up when it hits the ground). What do the lean force settings do?

 The following features or stunts are performed by professionals or under professional guidance, please do not re-enact the stunts performed in this game in real life instances…

Remember how we set the **Rotate CW** and **Rotate CCW** controls? This lean setting set indicates how much the control affects the character. Set it too high, and the character will spin like a top. Set it too low, and the player won't be able to accomplish tricks. The setting of 60 for the lean forces will allow for a complete backflip in the game off our jump. Try it out and see! When going up the ramp, lean back (using the left arrow), and hold it until you do a flip, release that arrow as you begin to come around to slow your flip and land on your wheels. If you land in a wheelie, release the throttle (the *D* key), and you'll bring down the front end. Play with it! You'll notice that using the throttle keys (*A* and *D*) will affect your aerial rotational speed too (due to the physics of torque). Now, this is a bit more fun, and with practice, the player will develop their skills! Much better… right? Please, feel free to go back and play with any and all of these physics settings to really get a feel for them.

Adding a new scene

Before we move out of basic Buildbox and go to intermediate techniques, let's cover one last topic. We're going to add a new scene that requires a choice.

When making a game, above all else you need to make the game fun to play. Too hard, and people get bored and give up. Too easy, and you have the same problem. If you really want people to play, you need to make it tough enough so that they can't just blow past everything on the first try, but hard enough so that some obstacles are so difficult that it takes multiple tries to get them right, and even then will take several more to master.

There's a great way to accomplish this, and that's by having a choice that seems obvious, but is not. We're going to create a scene that has a cave to drive through if they slow down and go over a small jump at moderate speed, but at high speed they can ride on top of the cave to a bigger jump. Eventually, we'll put a lot of small coin rewards inside the cave (which will make this the obvious choice). But every once in a while, a single large reward will appear for them to get if they take the large jump.

We'll add the rewards later, but let's go ahead and create the basic version of the cave level right now. First, (as before) copy the first ground-block to the clipboard using *Ctrl + C*.

In the scene selection window (at the bottom of Buildbox), click on the + Add button. This will add a blank scene. Now paste that first block using *Ctrl + V*. Now, using the same process as we used with the jump, create four more blocks, make the last one a small ramp, and extend our scene to match the following screenshot.

Time to bring in a new ground object. From the `Projects/RmblinRover/Ground` folder, let's bring in the `CaveBlock-Mars.png` file as an object in the same way we brought in our ground block. Before we adjust its size and position, let's adjust the collision shape for this object. In the **Objects** section of the asset library, select the **CaveBlock-Mars** object and open the **Collision Shape** editor. Edit the shape to match the following screenshot:

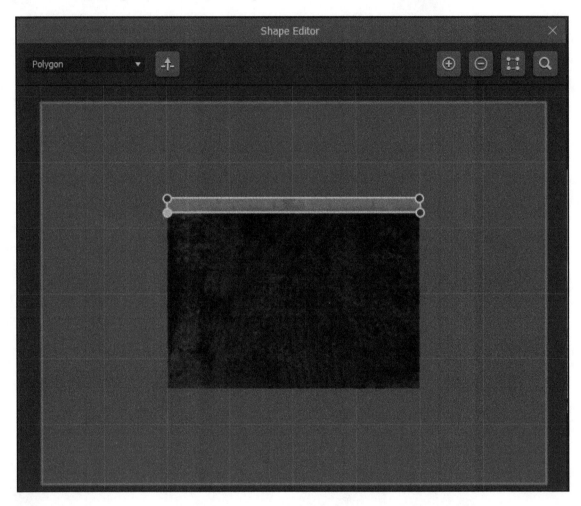

This way, the rover can drive through the cave, but will be destroyed if it collides with the top of the cave, and will be able to roll on top if they make the jump up there.

Now, let's adjust the size and position of this block before we duplicate it. Scale the block vertically, and position it to look like the following screenshot:

This is going to require some testing to get right. But we only want to test this scene, and not scene number 1. So, (even though it's already selected) select scene **2**, and hit the *S* key on your keyboard. This *solos* the number 2 scene. What that means is that all other scenes (except **Start** and **2**) are turned off, and the software will pretend they don't exist. This will make it much easier to test scenes to make sure they work in the way you want without having to waste time playing through the entire world. It's easy to tell if this is done because a little red line appears in all the scenes that are turned off, and a green line appears on the scenes that are on, as shown in the following screenshot:

Now test, adjust the cave-block, and retest until the rover just barely makes it on top of the cave-block at full speed. Then, you know it's positioned and scaled to a good size.

Now, copy the cave-block five times using our D key method, and rotate and scale the final two blocks so that they resemble the following screenshot:

Great! So now we have the top part of our cave with a big ramp! Now, let's make the bottom of our cave. First, let's duplicate the first block again on the screen (*Ctrl + C* and *Ctrl + V*). The scene will look no different. But take our word for it, there are now two starting blocks. If you hold down your shift key, and drag the block to the right, it will only move horizontally (and you won't have to worry about it being a different level than the starting block of the next scene). Drag this all the way to the end of the scene. It should look like this:

The problem we have is this: because we duplicated the first ground-block, we have a block that will be behind our cave-blocks when we duplicate it across the bottom. So in the Layers window, move the (currently highlighted) block up between the top **CavBlock-Mars** and the **Training Rover** layers.

We can also duplicate layers to the left (remember, using WASD keys duplicates objects in the corresponding direction). So, using the *A* key, duplicate the object to the left three times. Take the left-most block that you've just duplicated and move it down to almost the bottom of the visible area. You should now have this:

Almost there! Now, duplicate that block to the left (using the *A* key) until it overlaps with our original small ramp. Then use the block we just duplicated from to rotate and scale to form a small transition ramp up to the higher ground-blocks like this:

Now, you can un-solo the number 2 scene (using the same method we used to solo it in the first place), and you'll see that now your game has two distinct scenes that are completely playable, and challenging! Now, let's name them quickly so that as we get more scenes, we'll know what they are at a glance!

Naming your scene is relatively easy. Just select it in the scene selection window, and then enter the new names in the properties window. Let's name scene 1 **Big Jump** and scene 2 **The Cave**. The result will look like this:

Summary

WOW! We've come a long way, haven't we? All in one chapter as well. In this short time, we've learned how to set up our directory structure and prepare our environment to develop using naming conventions, and the **Game Creator** screen.

You've also learned more about the Game Mind Map, and used it to rename a world, and shortcut it to more easily test your game. We've also learned a great deal about the graphic formats for Buildbox, why they're used, and how to properly use them to make your game as resource-efficient as possible.

Backgrounds were interesting, and we got through all of the basics of instituting them with the principles of parallax. How did you enjoy seeing your background go by when testing the game? Pretty cool, right? But that's not all: we learned about image sequence animations, and how Buildbox uses them to make objects come to life.

We also got a chance to check out the basics of connections and parenting, and how they apply to a vehicle-based game. We also got to put our own graphics in the game and adjust the collision shapes so that they can work properly. We furthermore replaced all the graphics animations in our character, and even brought in an explosion for the destruction animation of our character.

We created two scenes with interesting and challenging obstacles to start our game, and we talked about the strategies of level design. We also got some tips and tricks to make obstacles more interesting and even give players choices by using collision shapes to make a cave (and a drivable top to the cave).

And finally, we learned how to set up our controls and how to test the game itself, and use that testing to adjust our obstacles to make them more usable. My, my, my… that was a lot to learn. This is a great time to take a break, and test your game some more to really get a feel for how to use the rover, and maybe even play around with the scenes we created to trick them out to your taste.

In the next chapter, Chapter 4, *Advanced World Design — Ramblin' Rover, Part 2*, we'll be moving on to more intermediate-level work within Buildbox. We'll create some physics-based obstacles to increase the challenge of our game, we'll again go over level-based versus endless games, and how to make your game level-based. We'll even create a secret level for the game! If you're unsure of anything we've covered so far, please go back and review, because the next chapter depends on everything you've learned here. You're well on your way!

4
Advanced World Design – Ramblin' Rover, Part 2

That was a lot of work in the last chapter, wasn't it? This chapter is going to take all of that up a notch. We're going to complete our Mars world, and even knock out two more worlds! If you're unsure of anything we covered previously, please take a moment to review it before we move forward. Ready? Ok, let's do this!

Making the rover jump

As we've mentioned before, we're making a hybrid game. That is, it's a combination of a motocross game, a platformer, and a side-scrolling shooter game. Our initial rover will not be able to shoot at anything (we'll save that feature for the next upgraded rover that anyone can buy with in-game currency). But this rover will need to jump in order to make the game more fun.

As we know, NASA has never made a rover for Mars that jumps. But if they did do that, how would they do it? The surface of Mars is a combination of dust and rocks, so the surface conditions vary greatly in both traction and softness. One viable way is to make the rover move in the same way a spacecraft maneuvers (using little gas jets). And since the gravity on Mars is lower than that on Earth, this seems legit enough to include it in our game.

While in our **Mars Training Ground** world, open the character properties for our **Training Rover**. Drag the animated PNG sequence located in our `Projects/RamblinRover/Characters/Rover001-Jump` folder (a small four-frame animation) into the `JumpAnimation` field. Now we have an animation of a jump-jet firing when we jump. We just need to make our rover actually jump. Your **Properties** window should look like the following screenshot:

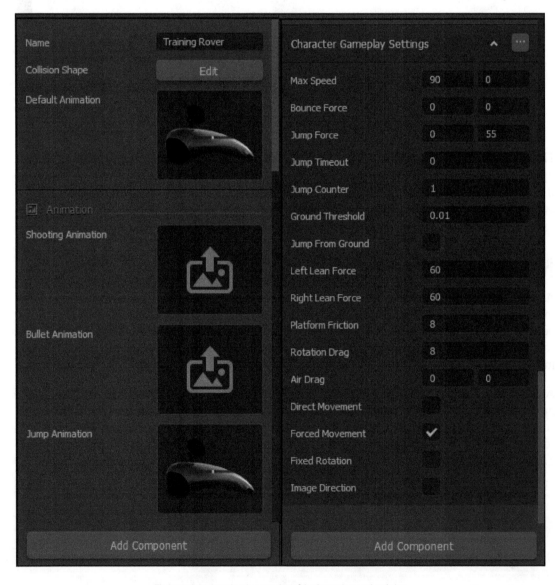

The image above shows the relevant sections of the character's properties window

As promised in the previous chapter, we're now going to revisit the **Character Gameplay Settings** section. Scroll the **Properties** window all the way down to this section. Here's where we actually configure a few settings in order to make the rover jump. The preceding screenshot shows the section as we're going to set it up. You can configure your settings similarly.

The first setting we are considering is **Jump Force**. You may notice that the vertical force is set to 55. Since our gravity is -20 in this world, we need enough force to not only counteract the gravity, but also to give us a decent height (about half the screen). A good rule is to just make our **Jump Force** 2x our **Gravity**.

Next is our **Jump Counter**. We've set it to 1. By default, it's set to 0. This actually means infinity. When the JumpCounter is set to 0, there is no limit to how many times a player can use the jump boost...they could effectively ride the top of the screen using the jump boost like a flappy bird control. So, we set it to 1 in order to limit the jumps to one at a time.

 There is also a strange oddity with Buildbox that we can exploit with this. The jump counter resets only after the rover hits the ground. But, there's a funny thing... the rover itself never actually touches the ground (unless it crashes), only the wheels do. There is one other way the jump counter can reset: by doing a flip. What this means is that once a player uses their jump up, the only way to reset it is to do a flip-trick off a ramp. An added level of difficulty and excitement to the game by using a quirk of the development software!

We could trick the software into believing that the character is simply close enough to the ground to reset the counter by increasing the **Ground Threshold** to the distance that the body is from the ground when the wheels have landed. But why? It's kind of cool that a player has to do a trick to reset the jump jets.

Finally, let's untick the **Jump From Ground** checkbox. Since we're using jets for our boost, it makes sense that the driver could activate them while in the air. Plus, as we've already said, the body never meets the ground. Again, we could raise the ground threshold, but let's not (for the reasons stated previously).

Awesome! Go ahead and give it a try by previewing the level. Try jumping on the small ramp we created that's used to get on top of our cave. Now, instead of barely clearing it, the rover will easily clear it, and the player can then reset the counter by doing a flip off the big ramp on top.

Physics obstacles

One really cool thing about platformer games are their physics-based obstacles. This would mean items such as teeter-totters, items that crumble, items that swing, and so on. Let's start with a basic pile of rocks with a ramp on it. Start by creating a new scene and copying our beginning ground block into it, as done before. Also, let's name this scene **Rock Jump**; duplicate an additional eight ground-blocks (so there's nine in total), and extend our scene bracket to match the length of the eight ground-blocks. You should have something like the following screenshot:

Now, remove the fifth and sixth block from the left to create a two-block gap just right of center. We duplicate the blocks all the way across the scene to make sure we have a level layer (rather than dragging and dropping across a gap). It's just a quicker way of doing things, but if you like, the same could be accomplished by dragging the fifth block over, and then continuing the duplication. Your exact process is your preference. Let's move on…

In the `Projects/RamblinRover/Ground` folder, you'll find the `rock001.png` file. Drag that to the stage as an object, and using the scale handle on the top-right of the box around the rock, scale it down so that it's just a bit taller than one of the wheels of the rover.

Quick note: if you hold down your *Shift* key while you scale, the rock will scale proportionally (both in horizontal and vertical directions equally).

Then, please position the rock on the ground so that your stage looks like this:

Now, let's make this a physics object. At the top of the **Properties** window for this object, you'll see a parameter called **Preset**. Set this to `Physics Object`. There are several different Presets that do various things to the object settings. All this one really does is change the **Object Type** parameter to **Physics**. We just wanted you to be aware of this **Preset** parameter for now… we'll get deeper into these a bit later. Also, we want this to destroy our character's body if it touches it, so change the **Destroy Type** to **Destroy Character** (as we did with the ground-blocks before). The results should look like the following screenshot:

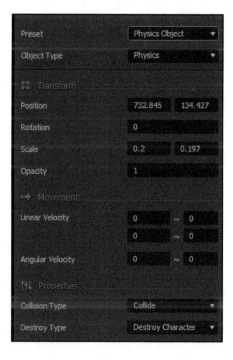

Now, let's make two more duplicates of the rock. We want to create a base for our ramp, and the objective of this is to make the rocks move, or even fall apart as the rover hits the ramp so that the player's strategy is to hit this obstacle as fast as possible. It should look somewhat like the following screenshot:

Before we actually add the plank for the ramp, we'll need to set up the rock's collision shape. As we did before for the character, adjust the collision shape for the rock object to match the following screenshot:

Notice that both the top and bottom of the rock are flat so that they can be evenly stacked.

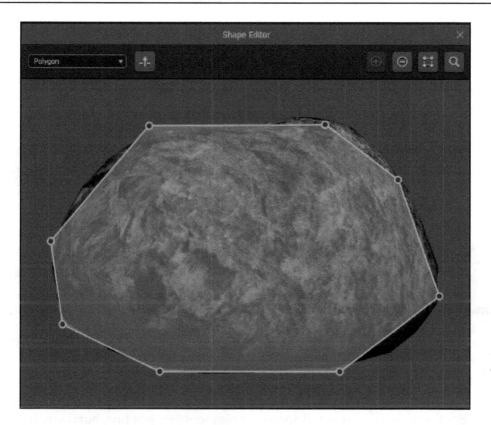

Now, we need an actual ramp. In the same folder as the `rock001.png` file, a file called `steel.png` is present. This is a simple metal texture that we can resize however we like. Go ahead and drag that onto our stage as another object. Again, make this a `Physics Object`, and set it so that it destroys the character on collision.

We can use this metal object to make a nice ramp by just squishing it down vertically, and sizing it a little bit horizontally. Then, if you grab the circle-shaped handle at the bottom-left of the object, you can rotate it. Use these controls, and position the ramp so it looks like this:

It's okay, for now, if none of these objects are directly touching each other. Remember, gravity will make them all fall upon generation, and they'll sit together (held by the same gravity).

Go ahead and test it out in the preview by soloing this scene and driving it a few times. You'll notice that if you take it at full speed, it holds together just fine, but if you try to slow down, the rover just pushes the ramp and rocks into the ditch… then the player is pretty much out of luck if they want to cross the ravine. Let's try something a bit crazier now…

We're going to use the same objects (the rock and steel) that we used in this scene. Go ahead and create a new scene called **Crazy Ramp 1**. It looks nuts, but based on what you just learned, please try to make this on your own. If you're not able to, we'll explain how to do it starting in the next paragraph. Alright, enough of the prelude…this is our next scene:

Overwhelmed? Don't worry, let's break it down for you a chunk at a time from left to right. First, let's just skip the ground-blocks...we're pretty sure you get that by now:

The first chunk is the initial ramp (the preceding screenshot). It's pretty much just a taller version of the ramp we made before, rocks (duplicated using the W key) that are all set to be `Physics Objects` that destroy the character upon collision. Then, the ramp is another steel object squished down and rotated in the same way we adjusted its shape for the last scene. Again, it's a Physics Object that destroys the character upon collision:

The next section is just a carbon copy of the ramp (pictured above). The only difference is that the rotation of the steel object is set to 0, and it's placed on top of both of the rock pillars.

The advantage of using a physics platform is that if the player stops or slows down while on the obstacle, the traction of the wheels on the ramp will grab it and either slide off the rocks, or make the entire structure fall down.

Finally, it's the T-ramp (in the preceding screenshot). These are both steel objects, and both are Physics Objects that destroy a character upon collision. One is squished horizontally, and the other is vertically scaled down. They are set so that the exact center of the top of the T (which happens to be marked by the vertical-scale handle) is placed in the center of the stem of the T. It will balance the top sheet well, until the rover hits it. Also, when the rover gets to this obstacle, the ramp will increase in pitch as the rover traverses it. Try it out using the Preview function!

Ok, so do you think you're ready to fly without a net to make another Crazy Ramp scene? Good. Make another scene called Crazy Ramp 2, and make it like the following screenshot:

Great job! Now, let's create some basic scenes for the beginning of the level. Remember how we created the original Big Jump and The Cave scenes? Use the same techniques to create these two scenes.

Name this first one Bumps.

And this one we'll call Simple Gap:

Now, let's make sure that the easiest levels are first (just for organizational sake). All you have to do is drag the scenes in the Scene Selection window to their proper positions. When complete, it should look like this:

There we go! So now we have a really good foundation for our first world. Some really simple scenes, and some crazier (at least crazier-looking) scenes. Remember, as it's our first world, it's meant to look cool, but be pretty easy. Now let's make a really fun scene that is one of the coolest things about a motocross game…a loop!

Making a loop

Ah, my favorite thing about motocross-type games…the loop. I don't know about you, but I've been looking forward to this section from the moment the book started. Before we start, let's explain the principle to you.

To complete a loop, the rover must be moving at high velocity so that its centrifugal force lets it defy gravity and keeps it on the ground even though the ground is upturned. So, we're going to need to build a long incline, and a steep downward ramp leading into the loop so that it can make it all the way around the loop without crashing down on its roof. But it still needs to be challenging, so it can't work just blindly. Firstly, what we're going to have to do is build the ramp so that in order to take it properly, the player will have to lean the vehicle so that after it comes off the top of the hump, it's airborne and needs to touch down in a way to help the velocity be high enough to carry it through the loop.

Secondly, as Buildbox is 2-dimensional, we'll have to build gaps in the ramp so that it can enter and exit the circle. But those gaps will need to be placed strategically, in such a way that it doesn't affect the rover's ability to traverse the loop.

Sound difficult? It isn't really…it just requires testing and adjusting to get it right.

First, let's build the ground. Go ahead and create a new scene called *Loop*, and make it look like this:

There we go…a nice smooth hump with a steep drop, and a ski-jump style ramp. Now we'll move on to the loop itself.

There's a strategy for making a loop. If you've ever looked closely at a roller coaster, only the highest-speed loops are actually circular. A loop that threatens to let you drop off at the top (low speed) needs to gradually get smaller. We're going to use the take-off ramp we've made to both take off (the top of it) the rover, and land the rover back safely (on the back side).

We could give you the settings for each individual piece of this loop. However, it's important to remember that this book is supposed to teach you how to *use* Buildbox, not just how to create Ramblin' Rover.

So, there is a PNG file in `Projects/RamblinRover/Ground` called `RawGroundBlock-Mars.png`. We'll use this to construct the platform for our loop. Drag this in as an object that destroys our character on collision (but not a Physics Object), duplicate it, and use scaling, rotation, and position to make the loop. Remember, test it using the soloing method and tweak it until you can (reliably) make it through the loop.

It should look something like the following screenshot:

Even Mars has gravity, and there's no way that loop is just going to sit there in mid-air. So let's build a framework as a decoration for it.

First, let's bring in two-more steel objects from our asset library. But change the **Collision Type** to NoCollide for both, and using the **Layers** window, place them under all other objects in the GamePlayLayer folder. Remember, we don't want to hit these supports as if they're obstacles. Position them as shown in the following screenshot:

Great! So now we've got our ground anchors for our structure, but we have no support structure. We want it to look kind of rickety, to add a bit more subconscious adrenaline for players…but this structure looks just downright unfeasible. Use the same technique to add some crossbeams to make it look like the following screenshot:

There we go!

As a side note, I had to do this twice because on the first try I inadvertently made it look like a pentacle. These things can happen sometimes, but it's important to note that we're not making the game *Doom* here. We also want to keep our potential user-base as wide as possible. For marketing purposes, know your audience. As we're dealing with geometry here, you may accidentally create a geometric shape that alienates a segment of your audience. Pay attention to these details; although sometimes controversy can be good free marketing, you also risk a boycott in this day and age.

So, now that the PC speech is over with…AWESOME! We have a really cool loop that looks kind of rickety, and everything works as expected in our easy level. "Too easy," you might say. Yes…if the whole goal is only to drive the rover around. But we have still to add our pickup coins (some of which will be pure death-bait), and our secret level portal!

Let's start with our secret level…

Making a secret level

Before we get to the level itself, we'll have to create a way to get there! We'll need a scene that pops up every so often in our game, but isn't readily-identifiable as the portal to our secret level. Let's start by duplicating an existing scene. If you select the **Rock Jump** scene, and use the D key on your keyboard, you'll create an exact copy of the whole scene. Finally, rename it Rock Jump Portal. Then, move the scene down (in the scene selection window) to the end of the list. It should look like the following screenshot:

Great! So upon entering the scene, the player will believe they are just entering another rock jump scene. But let's do something more interesting here. Make the scene look like the following screenshot (using the same techniques as before):

So, here's what this obstacle is all about: it's supposed to look like a simple platform held up by narrow sticks for the player drive across the top of. But if a player hits it just right, and reverses their thrust upon landing on top…they can make it fall over and bridge the gaps (just like the following screenshot):

Logic and effect assets

So, this is where we'll put our portal to a secret level. We'll need to use a Logic Asset to do this. Every type of Logic Asset has a different use:

- **Transform**: This is pretty much exactly how it sounds. Characters, objects, and enemies will be transformed (position, scale, or motion vector) when touching this. We'll use this inside our secret world.
- **Portal**: This is a way to teleport a character from one place to another. You can even use multiple portals to create clones. This can't be used with a motocross game (as only the character is teleported, not the wheels), so we'll use this much later in other examples.
- **Gatekeeper**: will only let a certain number of objects pass by it. It applies to all types of objects. So, say you clone your character, then want only one character on the screen. A gatekeeper could be used to only let one character by, and delete the rest.
- **Path**: A path object is just that…a path that an object will move along at a certain speed. It can be used for characters, enemies, and other objects. We'll use this one later.
- **Menu Jump**: A menu jump takes the player to a new screen or world when the character comes in contact with it. When you place a Menu Jump asset, a new output is placed on the world node in the Game Mind Map.

The player will need both observation and skill to get to the location we set up in the previous picture, so let's place our Menu Jump there. Now, grab a `MenuJump` asset from the **Logic** section of our **AssetLibrary** and place it as shown in the following screenshot:

Let's name this logic asset **Secret World**. You may remember from our demo game that it had such an item. This logic asset will take the player off the game screen to either a UI, or a different world. It does not show to the player in any visible way, so we're now going to have to place something else to let the player know that *something* is there.

Much like Logic Assets, each type of effect asset has a different result:

- **Light**: This is a point of light with a rudimentary lens flare that can also create an illusion of volumetric lighting (Buildbox calls them shadows, but a 3D artist would cringe at this name).
- **Trail**: This is an effect that can follow any object or character. It can be used to create an illusion of speed. It's basically a graphic that is deformed to match the motion of a character (for instance, jumping down the screen will make large arcs that follow the character).
- **Flag**: The flag effect is a graphic that appears to wave in a breeze as a basic flag would. We'll use this in just a bit.
- **Particle**: This is a generator. Particles can be used to imitate fairy dust, fire, smoke, or even sparks.
- **Mirror**: This is a great effect if you're on a wet surface. It creates a mirror image of everything around it. Be careful, though…it can be very resource intensive and run poorly on older mobile devices.

Go ahead and drag a `Particle` effect asset near the **MenuJump** we put on the screen earlier (don't place it on top of it yet). Name it Secret Indicator, and while in the Properties window, let's click on the **Edit** button for the **Emitters** parameter. You'll be confronted with the following interface:

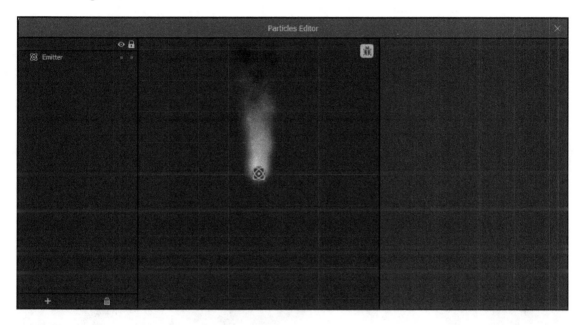

You should see an animated preview of some peculiar purplish smoke. Not exactly what we'll be going for. In this interface, we can add multiple emitters, and edit the emitters we currently use. We'll get deeper into this later for another world. But first, let's just change the parameters for our current emitter. Select it on the left side of the window by clicking **Emitter**. A whole lot of parameters will pop up. Let's check them out one by one:

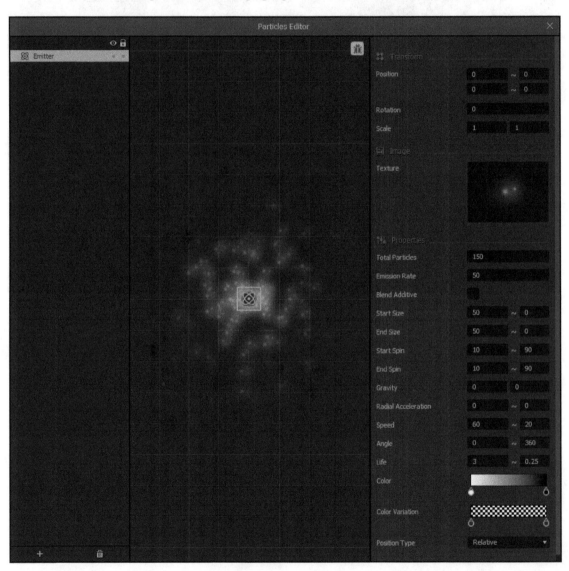

- **Position**: This is the position relative to the center of the emitter object on the stage. When setting up multiple emitters on one object, you may want them staggered. The top parameter is X, and the bottom is Y. The value next to each and separated with a ~ symbol is plus or minus (so you can randomize things within that space).
- **Rotation**: This allows the emitter to be rotated by degrees.
- **Scale**: Gives us the ability to make some emitters larger than others.
- **Texture**: Texture is the image (or sprite) that each particle will be made of.
- **Total particles**: The total number of particles allowed to be on screen at any given time.
- **Emission rate**: How many particles per second are created.
- **Start size**: How big each particle will be when created (again, the ~ symbol gives you the ability to randomize within constraints).
- **End size**: How big each particle will be at the end of its life.
- **Start spin**: The amount of rotation each particle will have when created.
- **End spin**: The amount of rotation each particle will have upon deletion.
- **Gravity**: How much each particle will be attracted in any given direction (very useful for things such as water and sparks).
- **Radial acceleration**: How much each particle will speed up (with a positive number) or slow down (with a negative number) as it gets further away from the emitter.
- **Speed**: How fast each particle initially moves when generated.
- **Angle**: The angle of each particle's movement.
- **Life**: How long each particle will last (in seconds).
- **Color**: The tint of the texture of each particle over its life.
- **Color variation**: How much each particle will vary its color over its life.
- **Position type**: How each particle is positioned.

Match your emitter settings to the preceding screenshot. As you change each setting, see how it affects the outcome. For instance, notice that changing the angle to 0 ~ 360 emits particles at a 0 angle, but randomizes them across the entire 360 degree area around the emitter.

When finished, close the emitter editor, and position the emitter directly over the menu jump we placed earlier to match the following screenshot:

We'll come back here later. But for now, let's create…

A whole new world

Back at the Game Mind Map, right-click in the blank area, and create a new world. Name this new world Mars Secret World and duplicate the parameters from the Mars Training Ground's properties. After all, we're still on Mars, so we want the same physics. Now, duplicate (using the WASD keys) the **Game Field UI** node, and the **Game Over UI** node. Name these, and connect them as shown in the following screenshot:

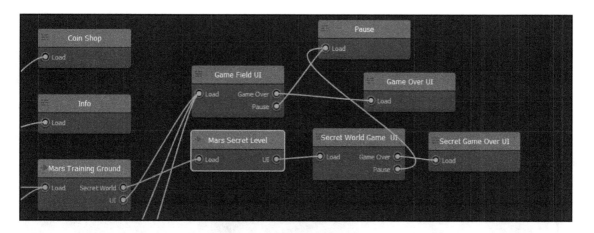

The reason we duplicated our UIs (rather than using the originals) is that when the character is destroyed, we don't want the level to start over. We'd like the player to go back to Mars. So, let's set that up really quickly. We'll get deeper into UIs later, but for now, double-click on the **Secret Game Over UI**.

Now, just select the **Restart** button, and set the **Function** parameter to `Default`. This will give us an output on this node back at the Game Mind Map. Go back to the Game Mind Map and connect it up as shown in the following screenshot:

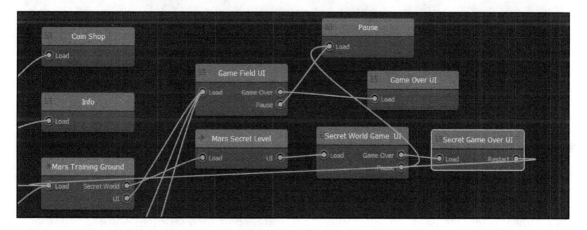

Awesome! So our basic structure is down for our secret world. Now, let's actually make our world...

Open up the **Mars Secret Level** and bring in the `InnerCave.png` from `Projects/RamblinRover/Backgrounds` as a background. We don't need to worry about parallax on this level because we're underground. Now, set up the character as we outlined before (using scale and connections) so that it looks like the following screenshot. If you have trouble, go back to the section in `Chapter 3`, *Your First Game — Ramblin' Rover, Part 1*, where we talk about connections and how they work to review. Don't forget to bring in the character objects from the Asset Library (so you don't duplicate resources). Also, remember to set the boundaries for the character complete with death at the bottom, and restriction on the top:

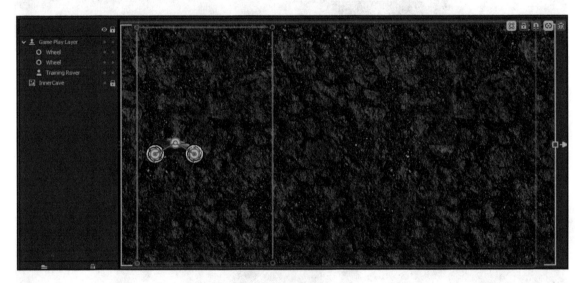

There's one more thing we need to do (which we haven't covered before) to make a motocross character work properly. And that's to set the properties of the connections. If you click on the connection lines themselves, you'll want to set the properties to a **Speed** of 50, a **Torque** of 200, and enable the **ButtonActivated** parameter by ticking the checkbox for it. These are the settings that actually let the wheels spin when you use controls. Without these, the character will just land and sit on the ground, no matter what you do with the controls.

We want this level to be pretty hard. It will ultimately be a long string of nothing but rewards…and a ton of them. So, we want to make it more difficult to traverse with lots of traps. For that reason, we'll have ceilings, and narrow gaps to traverse. So, make a total of four scenes that look like this using the **CaveBlock-Mars** asset we already have in the library:

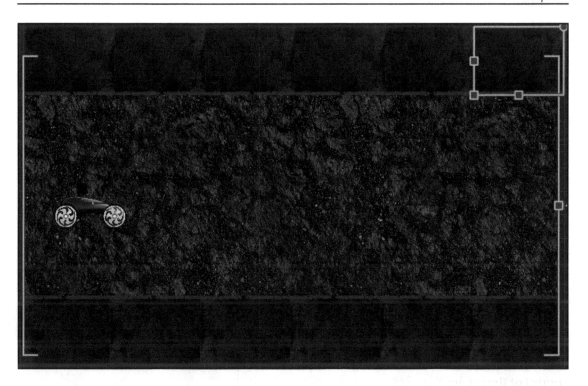

Hump-Stairs. This scene is so that if they come in too fast, they'll hit the ceiling. But if they come in too slow, they'll tumble down the stairs and crash:

Cave Jump 001. Here, we'll take advantage of the player's need for speed, and give them the opportunity to perform a flip:

Crazy Bumps is a level designed to set the player off balance and struggle to maintain control of the rover:

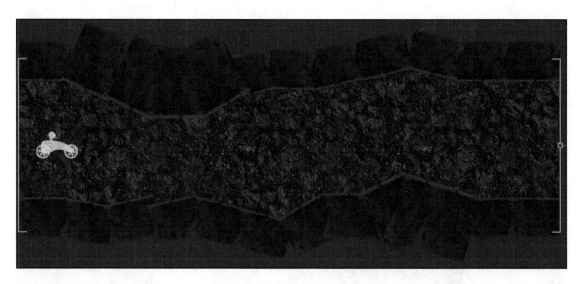

Great! So now we have our base for our first four scenes. We'll build some more, but let's place some lights to make this more interesting…

From the Effects section of the Asset Library, bring in a **Light**. Set the **Color** of the light to a very desaturated yellow (meaning a pale yellow) with a brightness of about 50% in the color requestor. Place the light as shown in the following screenshot on the **Start** scene with the settings indicated in the screenshot:

Before we test this, copy this light and paste it as shown in our other three scenes:

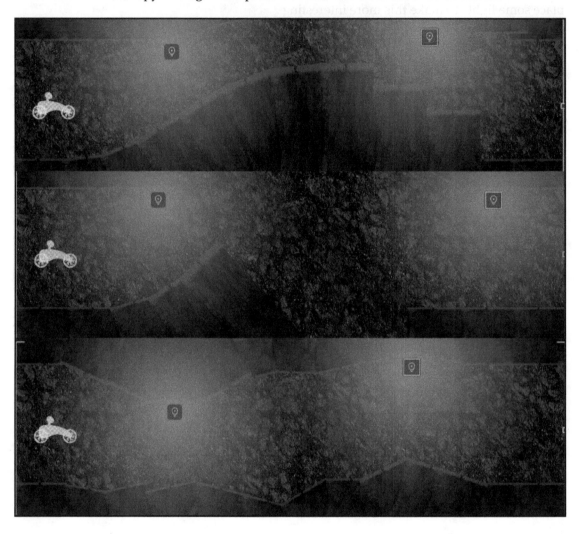

Awesome! Give it a try now. Remember, you can jump straight to this world by setting the output from the **Start** node to the **Load** of the **MarsSecretLevel** node in the Game Mind Map.

Let's create two more scenes. These will have tougher dynamic obstacles…

Dynamic obstacles – part 1

In this first scene, we'll make a platform that moves quickly up and down. This motion will create a *bumper* to knock the rover up and over another obstacle. Create a new scene and call it Bumper 001. Let's just make the first chunk of this scene for now. Set up objects as shown in the following screenshot (the squares with a rotating arrow in the middle are **Transform** Logic assets):

You're about to learn how transform objects work. Let's start by giving some default motion to our Steel object. Select the Steel platform and change its vertical **Linear Velocity** to −15. This will start its motion downward. The settings should match the following screenshot:

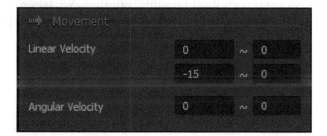

Now select the Transform object beneath the Steel platform. In the **Properties** window for this object, we can set up the object it affects, and just how it affects it. Please set the settings as indicated in the following screenshot (and then we'll tell you what it all means):

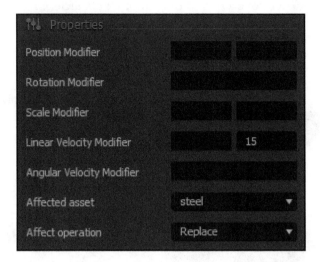

So, as we know a Transform object is one that transforms what touches it in some way. However, it will only affect one object, and *that* is the object that must activate it. So, in the **Affected asset** parameter, we select `steel`. You may notice that this drop-down menu only lists one instance of each type of object. This is because it will affect *any* instance of that type of object that touches it.

We can also set the **Affect operation** to `Add` to existing values, `Multiply` the existing value by something, or simply `Replace` the value with a new one. So, we selected `Replace`. Finally, all we want to change is the vertical **Linear Velocity Modifier**, so we set the new value to `15`. Set up the other Transform object in the same way, except set this **Linear Velocity Modifier** to `-15`.

What this will all do is when the items are generated, the steel platform will move down. Upon touching the lower Transform object, it will move up…then down again when it touches the upper Transform object. It will do this infinitely. So, when your rover rolls over it just right, the rover will be shot up and over the next obstacle, which looks like this:

Notice that we also placed some `RawGroundBlock-Mars` objects along the sides of some of the blocks to create collision zones (because our underground block only has collision on the top part of its shape). Test and adjust this so that it's nearly impossible, but if you time it *just right*, you will go over the obstacle at full throttle.

Now, use all of these principles to create a new scene called *Crusher 001* like this:

The first five steel blocks and the very last one will begin with a vertical **Linear Velocity** of -10. The other four blocks will begin with a vertical **Linear Velocity** of 10. All of the Transform objects will Multiply the vertical velocity value by -1. Using Multiply instead of a static value gives the same result, but since we have so many blocks to worry about we can now edit speed (if we desire) just by changing the blocks, and not every single Transform object. What we've ended up with here is a cascading series of crushing pillars that force you to move at full throttle through here and to time it just right.

Now, go back and add lights, as we did before, to these scenes. It's time to add some rewards and death-bait.

Rewards and pickups

Back in the **Start** scene for our Mars Secret Level, let's drag in all of the images (because it's an image sequence) from the Projects/RamblinRover/Pickups/Coins/Normal/Comp 1 folder, as an **Action**.

Actions (compared to Objects) are how we create unique pickups and...well, actions. These might include temporary invincibility, killing all enemies, rewards, and healing damage.

Select your new coin pickup from the Actions section of the Asset Library, and we'll work with the properties a bit. Let's take a quick look at these properties one by one (starting with **Action Type** because you should have a firm handle on **Collision Shape** and **Default Animation** by now):

- **Action Type**: This is kind of a preset option. Here, you can set it for the various types of pickup that Buildbox has to offer. Let's set this to Coin.
- **Action Animation**: This is mostly useful if we're going to do Invincibility, or Kill All Enemies for our **Action Type**. With this, we could project a wave across the whole screen, or change our character to a glowing version. Of course, we could use it for coins to show the amount, but we want to stay resource light, so we'll leave this blank.
- **Animation Placement**: You can place the **ActionAnimation** on the Character, on the pickup, or across the whole screen with these options. As we're not using the **ActionAnimation** right now, leave this alone.
- **Animation Behavior**: This setting dictates whether our **Action Animation** is overlaid on our **Animation Placement** (for instance, on top of the Character), or completely replaces it. It's irrelevant here.

- **Animation Repeat**: A setting to make the **ActionAnimation** repeat, or play only once. Again, it's not relevant because we have no **ActionAnimation**.
- **Idle Sound**: The sound played when the pickup is just sitting on the screen. (We'll come back to sounds later.)
- **Start Sound**: The sound played when the pickup is picked up. (We'll come back to sounds later.)
- **End Sound**: The sound played at the end of the pickup duration. (We'll come back to sounds later.)
- **Reward Coins**: This is where we can set how many coins are attained by touching the pickup. Let's set this to `10`.
- **Show coin reward**: Here, we can set if the number of coins is displayed when the coins are picked up. Let's tick this checkbox.
- **Reward Points**: How many points the pickup is worth. This is a coin pickup, so leave this at points.
- **Duration**: How long before the affect ends (mostly used for invincibility-type affects). However, we can also use this to play an **End Sound** after a delay, so set this to `0.1`.
- **Appearance Chance**: How likely this pickup is to show up on our game field. This is great for giving us some variety (even though our game will repeat scenes). Since this is a low-level reward, set this to `80` (meaning 80%).
- **Camera Shake**: How long (in seconds) the screen appears to shake when the pickup is touched. Set this to `0.1`.
- **Camera Flash**: How long the screen turns white in the event of pickup. Also set this to `0.1`.

Now that we've set up our low-level coin pickup object, let's bring in our high-level pickup object. Drag in all of the images (image sequence again) in the `Projects/RamblinRover/Pickups/Coins/Red/Comp 1` folder as an **Action**. For this Action, set up the settings in the same way, except for the **RewardCoins** and **Appearance Chance**; make this worth `100` coins with a `25` chance of appearance.

When we place these rewards on the game field, all we have to do is **Scale** them to look good. Make their scale 0.3 in both axes. Place them around our Mars maps to look like the following screenshots:

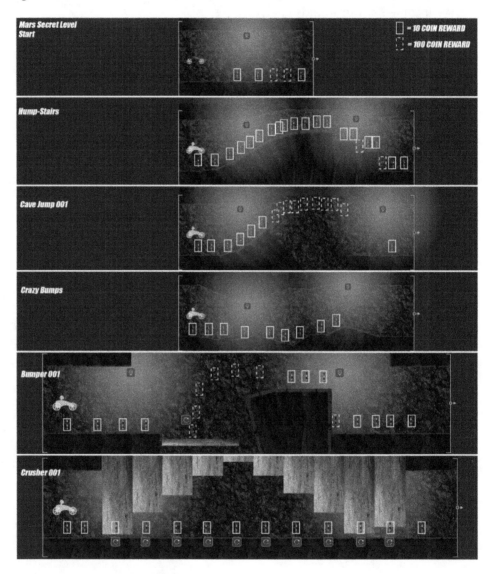

Ok, so none of the secret level's pickups are death-bait. But this level is already hard enough. Let's do the **Mars Training Ground** now:

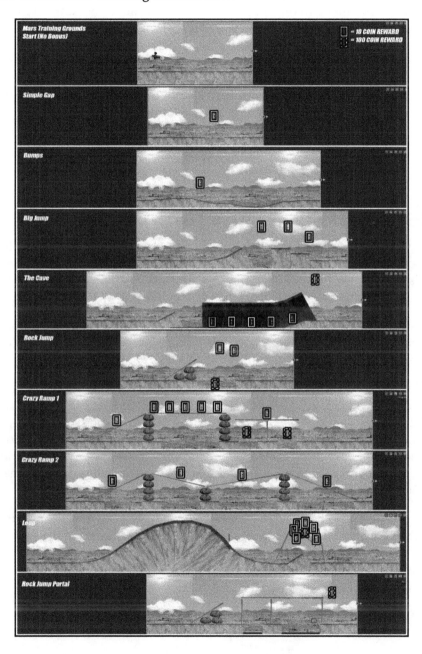

You may notice that there are FAR fewer coin pickups in the standard level. Well, this is because the player should get a big reward for finding that secret level. Also, it makes a player hungrier for bonuses, so the death-bait that we've laid in this scene will be far more effective. Never underestimate the greed of a player. The death-bait includes pickups that will cause a player to exhaust their rocket-thrusters, take physics obstacles in un-passable ways, make them fall into gaps, try to fall through the loop, take alternate routes, and even skip over the bonus level. It'll be harder for them to understand that the reds are mostly used for death-bait because they only show up 25% of the time. Try it out! You'll find yourself trying for the death-bait (even though you know what it is).

Now that you're an expert at creating worlds for our motocross game, let's create two more quick worlds.

Different worlds = different physics?

That's right, we can set up different rules of physics for each world. But it goes further than that; each world is almost like its own version of the game. We'll have to replace backgrounds, re-scale the parts of our character, fit them together, and so on. It's essentially like going back to square one of our Mars Training Ground.

Our next two worlds will be Gliese 581D and Kepler 186F. These are real exoplanets found by astrophysicists, so we can guess at what the physics and scenery should be (with some embellishments courtesy of imagination).

Gliese 581D was discovered in 2007 and is the fourth planet from the star Gliese 581. It's also on the edge of what's known as the *habitable zone*. It's theorized that it's a primeval environment with active volcanos. It is also nearly seven times the size of Earth, and only about 20 light-years away from Earth. So, it's going to have some very strong gravity. We'll also make the surface have more traction (as it's going to be mostly rock), very sparse (if any) vegetation, and smokey. We'll also put in an alien enemy (although this enemy will be little more than an obstacle for this world, and will be pretty passive).

Kepler 186F was discovered in 2015. It's much further away from Earth at around 490 light-years. The cool thing is though that it's both in the habitable zone from the star Kepler 186, and it's about the same size as Earth. So, we're going to make this a lush planet with similar physics to Earth. But since it's Earth-like, we're going to make a very aggressive indigenous life-form. Let's get started…

Rename World 2 Gliese 581D and World 3 Kepler 186F. Use the knowledge you've accumulated thus far to create the following scenes in these worlds. If you're unsure of anything, feel free to open the completed `RamblinRover-Chapter4` project file and see how things are set up.

Gliese 581D

Let's set up the physics for this world. As we mentioned, traction and gravity would be more powerful. So, let's set the vertical **Gravity** force to -75 (as opposed to -20 on Mars). Also, set the **Friction** to 60 (which was 30 on Mars). Now, let's create the scenes...

Start

Here's the opening scene's characteristics:

- The assets are located in appropriate folders for the backgrounds. Don't forget to use parallax.
- The smokey texture is on top of everything (like the lens reflections) and its **Speed** should be 2.0.
- Use the Mars cave-blocks for the ground of this world.
- Make it look like the following screenshot:

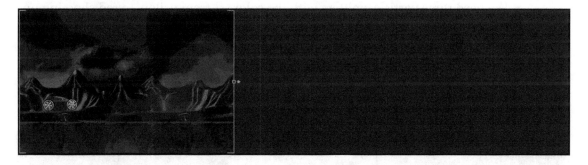

Bumps

This is an easy scene that sets the rover a bit off-balance:

- The `BareTree` asset should be set as a `Decoration`
- There should be only one 10-credit pickup
- Make it look like the following screenshot:

Lava jump

Now we get to make our scenery more interesting by jumping over lava pits:

- The `Lava` object is set as a `Decoration` (as we'll die falling through it anyway).
- We need three particle emitters with the color set from yellow to red shooting up to look like lava bubbling up. Boost the emission rate to `200`, and change the angle ~ to `45`.
- We need three 10-credit pickups.
- This jump should be nearly impossible (the next rover will be faster).
- Make it look like the following screenshot:

Moosquatch 001

This scene is where everything changes. Players will absolutely have to get the next rover to get by these obstacles. On top, there is our first enemy, and below there are impassable rocks. The next rover will have a gun to eliminate either of these obstacles. Additionally, when the rover gets onto the ramp, two of the sections will slowly slide down to the lower level. This is how everything looks:

To create an enemy, it's really like any other object. Just drag in all of the Moosquatch images in the sequence of him standing as an object. Then just set him to Enemy in the **Preset** parameter. This will set up his collision behaviors properly. And of course, the rocks are physics objects.

The top two sections of ramp (the nearly level one, and the one before it) have a **LinearVelocity** of 2.5 (horizontal) and -10 (vertical) for the nearly level one, and 1.25 x -5 for the one before it. Now we have to make them drop only when the rover gets close.

For this, click the **Add Component** button, and choose Wake Up. Set the **Wake Up** to Distance Based, the **Wakeup Distance** to 150, and **Sleep** to Disabled. Do this for both blocks. What this will do is make the **Linear Velocity** we set these blocks to activate once the rover is within 150 pixels of the blocks. Effectively, we've created an elevator to the lower level.

Teeter secret portal

This one is pretty straight forward. If they ride the left-side of the teeter down, the player can back up and hit the secret portal (with a particle emitter on top of it as before). Follow this screenshot as a guide:

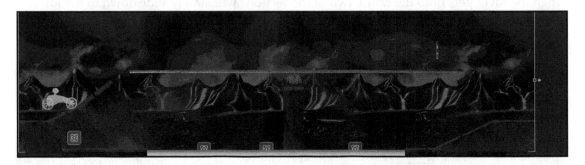

Bump jump

Bump Jump also looks pretty straightforward. The steel ramp we set in place has a wake up that will move it up at a rate of 20. Then, two transform assets are placed to move it back down by -20, and then stop it back in place. This creates a bumper that gives the player a little extra boost in their jump. Take a look at the following screenshot as a guide:

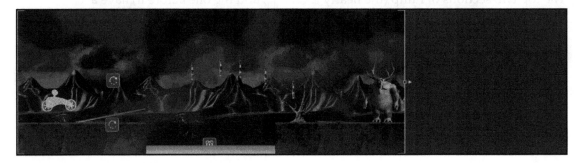

Conveyer chop

Alright, ready to put what you've learned to the test? Remember that transform objects affect all instances of an asset that touches them. So, we've set up two transform objects (one at each end), and two rows of steel plates with some gaps. The top row plates all have a horizontal **Linear Velocity** of 15 while the bottom row's plates are at -15. The transform on the right sets the **Position Modifier** to the same vertical value as the bottom row, and its **Linear Velocity Modifier** to -15 (sending the object to the bottom row and moving it along with the rest of the bottom row). The one of the left does the opposite (moves the bottom row objects up to the top row, and sends them to the right). This creates what looks and acts like a conveyor belt. Set all of the steel plates to `No Destroy`, and this will make it chop up the rover if it ends up pinched between the two directions, then it will be destroyed when it lands in the lava, or the body on the ground. Again, it should resemble the following screenshot:

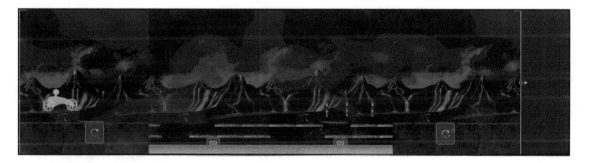

Shaman Moosquatch

In this level, we're going to work with a path object to make it look like a shaman version of our Moosquatch is levitating our rover over a lava obstacle.

Create the preceding scene (with our Shaman Moosquatch image sequence for the enemy). For the particles on the path, we'll use a green emitter on the left, a blue one on the right, and the same on the Shaman Moosquatch's hands (this will make it look more like he's controlling the path).

Drawing a path is pretty simple. Once it's dragged to the starting point, just drag the little + icon to the next place where you'd like a point. You can continue this to draw out the full path as shown above. To create a new point in the middle of a line, just click the + icon sitting in the halfway point and drag it to where you'd like it.

The **Search Radius** is how many pixels around the path will be the attraction area (how close an object needs to be in order to be brought to the path). Set this to 30. The **Speed** is how fast an object moves along the path (also should be 30), and the **Attraction Force** is how strongly an object is pulled to the path (set to 50). Too weak, and you'll fly off the path. Too strong, and an object won't be able to leave the path.

Now just make sure that **Keep Velocity** is un-ticked, the **Play Mode** is single (versus looped), and that the **Affected Asset** is set to Characters. Now, when your rover hits the path, it'll be levitated across the screen in a crazy path.

Gliese secret level

This one is pretty easy. Just duplicate the Mars Secret Level, but change the physics settings to match Gliese. Why? We're going to make the player feel complacent by giving them the same secret level on the second world (with only changing physics). Then, on the third world, everything will be completely different and shock them a bit. The Game Mind Map should look like the following screenshot:

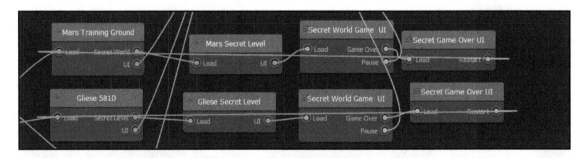

Kepler 186F

Consider this world the final test of the skills you've learned in this chapter. Remember, if there's anything you're unsure of, you can either refer back to how we did similar operations thus far, or check out the `RamblinRover-Chapter4` project file. The physics settings for this world are as follows:

- **Vertical gravity:** -55
- **Time warp:** 90
- **Friction:** 50
- **Bounce:** 0.5

Start

This world is completely different. There are a ton of background layers in here, but hey…by now, you're an expert at parallax, right? All of the buildings are organized so that 001 is behind 002 and so on. Create these scenes based on the following screenshots:

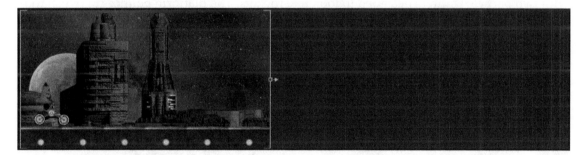

Basic jump

This is the first time a player will encounter a shooting enemy. We've taken these screen shots in connection mode, because this world is all about connections and using them effectively. The enemy is `psychLopseShooting`. You'll notice that we have something connected to the end of the gun. This is the `LaserShot` asset. The PNG for it is in the `Characters` folder for this project. The scene looks like the following screenshot:

Select the `Enemy Bullet` **Preset** for this `LaserShot`. Now, all you have to do is add a `Spawner` component to this object. Now, it will repeatedly shoot so long as the enemy shooting it is still alive. Let's set the **Spawn Rate** to `0.5` (or every half-second) to match the animation of the enemy's *kick* from the gun firing.

Floating alien

Ok, here, we take it to the next level. This time, the alien is standing on a steel platform asset with two particle emitters designed to look like rockets. The platform bounces between four transform assets to create a floating path. Play with it to make sure the platform floats between the transform objects:

Walking alien

This takes a little bit of thinking outside the box, actually quite literally. The walking version of psychlopse is really a tall box (in terms of physics analysis). What if it hits a bump? It may just topple over. To quote William Bell from the series *Fringe*, "Physics is a..." ok, let's paraphrase...physics can be tough. So, it's parented to a steel platform that is set as a physics object. Not only that, but the steel platform's **Opacity** is set to 0. That way, the player never sees it. Also, the steel platform now acts like a sled (with a very low profile, so it doesn't easily topple over).

The sled is then a child of another small steel block (really, it doesn't matter what object you use) that is out of view, and set to move across the playing field just above the view from right to left. Now, the sled is dragged along the ground (because it's a physics object), and the enemy looks as though it's walking. This is how all walking enemies are created in Buildbox. He'll follow the terrain, and progressively become an impediment to our rover. Just set the speed of the master object, and the speed of our image sequence's playback to match a reasonable walking rate without *Scooby-Doo* (or *skating*) feet:

Massive Mech

This really is a scene that will make any player gulp with terror, with a massive robot that shoots in nearly all directions. This is just an over-bloated version of everything else we've done in this world: a walker with four guns that shoot at different rates. The top gun is nearly continuous (as it's a Gatling-style gun), while the bottom gun is around 1.5 seconds, with the other guns falling squarely in the middle. Just adjust the velocities of the bullets to match their angles (it may take some tweaking). You'll find that it's a much easier scene to make than it looks:

Tunnel_001

Take a breath...now we just rinse and repeat in different ways. Here, we're going to get players used to a tunnel environment on Kepler for the bonus levels. The same background we'll use as a full background in our secret level, we'll use as a decoration here. You'll find the `SteelPlate.png` file in our `backgrounds` folder. Also, our secret level portal will be in the bunker with the shooting alien (complete with the tell-tale particle emitter). It should resemble the following screenshot:

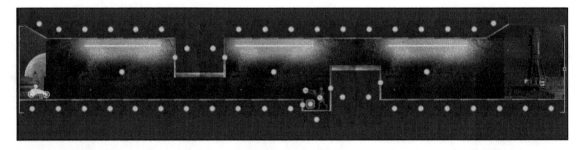

Tunnel002

Again, this is rinse and repeat. This is just another tunnel level with another massive mech. This way we can switch up our scenery often enough to break up the monotony a bit. So, our final tunnel should look like this:

Kepler secret level

This is where things switch up a bit. There's no real enemies (after all, it's a bonus level), but a rocket platform (like our floating alien) that we ride instead, more bumpers (like Gliese), and even a scene where we have to back up (also like Gliese).

There's some things to notice before we show you the image:

- The rocket platform is a wake platform with particle emitters parented to it. Also, there is a transform to stop it at the end.
- The pillars are unpassable by any rover except the third rover, which will be able to fly via a flappy-bird style of flight.
- The Bump Crusher scene has only two transform attributes stretched to cover all of the bumpers.
- The Pinball scene has 100-credit death-bait (red) pickups buried in each corner of the platforms.

We advise you open up the `RamblinRover-Chapter4` project in the downloadable content to examine these scenes. Build the bonus level so it looks like the following images:

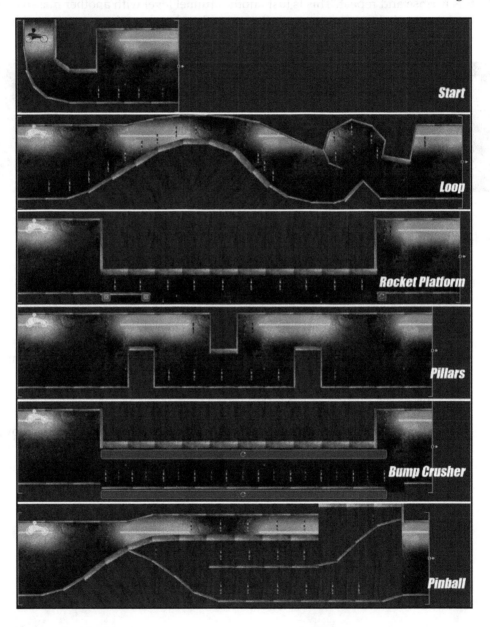

Summary

If we said *WOW* at the end of the last chapter, we'll give a *HOLY COW* to this one. All of the playable levels of our game are now complete. Take a break. Let it all sink in. This was an enormous deluge of information. Believe it or not, we've only just begun! In the next chapter, we'll cover some advanced features to polish our playable levels, create our next two rovers, complete our UIs and menus, and get on the road to making money with a monetization structure!

Brace yourself, take a deep breath, and let's do this!

5
Menus, UIs, Sound, and More! – Ramblin' Rover, Part 3

So, we've pretty much completed the game field (except for some minor items that we'll address quite soon). But believe it or not, we're only halfway there! In this chapter, we're going to finally create our other two rovers, and test and tweak our scenes with them. We'll set up all of our menus, information screens, and even a coin shop where we can use in-game currency to buy the other two rovers, or even use real-world currency to short-cut and buy more in-game currency. And speaking of monetization, we'll set up two different types of advertising from multiple providers to help us make some extra cash. Or, in the coin-shop, players can pay a modest fee to remove all advertising!

Ready? Well, here we go!

We got a fever, and the only cure is more rovers!

So now that we've created other worlds, we definitely need to set up some rovers that are capable of traversing them. Let's begin with the optimal rover for Gliese. This one is called The K.R.A.B.B. (no, it doesn't actually stand for anything...but the rover looks like a crab, and acronyms look more military-like).

Go ahead and drag all of the images in the Rover002-Body folder in as a characters. Don't worry about the error message. This just tells you that only one character can be on the stage at a time. The software still loads this new character into the library, and that's all we really want at this time anyway. Of course, drag the images in the Rover002-Jump folder to the **Jump Animation** field, and the LaserShot.png file to the **Bullet Animation** field.

Set up your K.R.A.B.B. with the following settings:

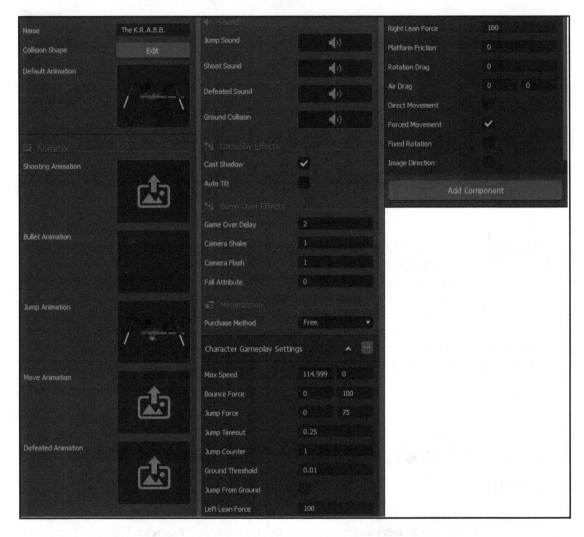

For the **Collision Shape**, match this:

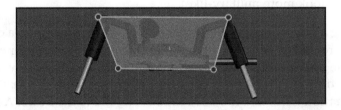

In the **Asset Library**, drag the K.R.A.B.B. above the Mars Training Rover. This will make it the default rover. Now, you can test your Gliese level (by soloing each scene) with this rover to make sure it's challenging, yet attainable. You'll notice some problems with the gun destroying ground objects, but we'll solve that soon enough.

Now, let's do the same with Rover 003. This one uses a single image for the **Default Animation**, but an image sequence for the jump. We'll get to the bullet for this one in a moment, but set it up like this:

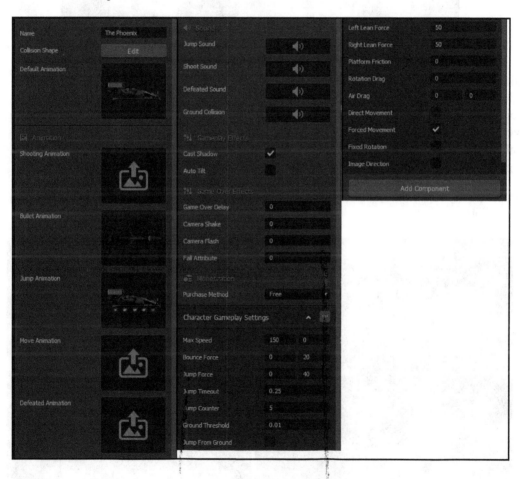

And the **Collision Shape** should look like this:

You'll notice that a lot of the settings are different on this character, and you may wonder what the advantage of this is (since it doesn't lean as much as the K.R.A.B.B.). Well, it's a tank, so the damage it can take will be higher (which we'll set up shortly), and it can do multiple jumps before recharging (five, to be exact). This way, this rover can fly using flappy-bird style controls for short distances. It's going to take a lot more skill to pilot this rover, but once mastered…it'll be unstoppable. Let's move on to the bullet for this rover. Click on the **Edit** button (the little pencil icon) inside the **Bullet Animation** (once you've dragged the `missile.png` file into the field), and let's add a flame trail.

Set up a particle emitter on the missile, and position it as shown in the following screenshots:

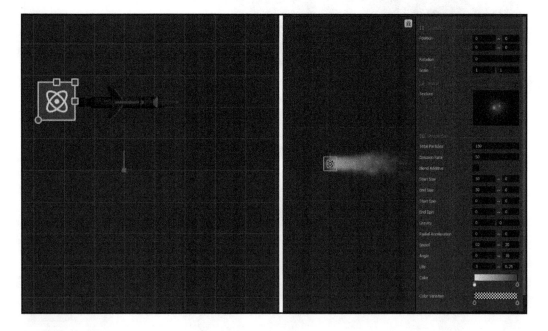

The image on the left shows the placement of the missile and the particle emitter. On the right, you can see the flame set up. You may wonder why it is pointed in the opposite direction. This will actually make the flames look more realistic (as if they're drifting behind the missile).

Very cool! Now we can drag this rover to the top of our **Asset Library**, and test it on Kepler. Again, make sure the level is very tough, but somewhat attainable. Remember, we want people who've mastered the Phoenix to still have a challenge here.

What in the heck did we just do?

Well, we just created two new rovers. Each one is faster than the one before, which we achieved by changing the **Max Speed** parameter. Furthermore, we made our two new rovers capable of shooting by simply adding a **Bullet Animation**.

We also took into account how each of these rovers would act in the real world. Obviously, the K.R.A.B.B. is thinner, and lighter, so it will rotate much faster (using **Left Lean Force** and **Right Lean Force**) than our other rovers. And the Phoenix is basically a tank, so it will be heavier, and not as nimble. But it carries a lot more rockets, and has the ability to fly for a limited range.

Ok, now let's set up damage so that our shots don't destroy ground objects, and our tank can take more damage (and deal more damage) than our other rovers.

Damage and health

By default, everything has 1 health point and deals 1 damage point. So, when you shoot your bullets, they will only deal 1 damage. By adding additional health to ground objects, we'll be able to make them (to all intents and purposes) indestructible. Similarly, by adding more damage to the missiles for our Phoenix rover, it will effectively kill objects that have higher health easier. Here's how it's done.

Let's begin with all of the ground objects (GroundBlock-Mars, CaveBlock-Mars, RawGround, Steel, and GroundBlock-Kepler). Repeat the following procedure for all of these blocks:

1. Select the object in the **Asset Library**.
2. At the bottom of the Properties window, click on the **Add Component** button.
3. Add both Damage and Health to each object. This is because our tank will have more health, but we still want it destroyed if it flips over. So, we have to make the ground very lethal by adding damage, and resilient to bullets by adding health.
4. Increase both the **Damage** and **Health** values to 999999, while leaving any **Delay** values at 0.

Ok! So now we've made all of our ground objects invincible and very deadly. Don't worry, this won't destroy our wheels. Ground objects can only destroy our character because we already set the **Destroy Type** to Destroy Character.

Now, there are only two characters that are capable of destroying anything: the K.R.A.B.B. and the Phoenix. The K.R.A.B.B. is easy enough. It only has one health and one damage (which it already has by default), so we can leave it alone. The Phoenix is a tank that shoots missiles, so we'll need to set its **Health** to 3, and its **Damage** to 5. Use the same procedure as before to set these values.

There's just one more thing to set up now. That MechWalking object is a giant deadly beast, right? Yes, but it's also a giant *TOUGH* deadly beast. Let's leave the **Damage** alone. It already shoots a barrage of bullets at our characters. But let's increase the **Health** to 6. This way, the K.R.A.B.B. will have to shoot it 6 times to kill it, but the Phoenix will only have to shoot it twice.

And there we have it! All of our Damage and Health values are set up in our game. Give it a try with each of the rovers by just moving whatever rover you'd like to use to the top of the characters list. You'll find that it's much more playable and fun now. When you're done, set the order of the rovers to Training Rover, the K.R.A.B.B., and finally, the Phoenix. This will set up their order properly for later. Now, let's move on to the final touch in our game fields.

Creating a starting flag

Setting up a starting flag is really an easy proposition. Choose any of the three maps (it doesn't matter which one you do first, as all three worlds will have a starting flag). Also, remember to select the Start scene within that world. Add a steel object as a decoration (no collide, no destroy) and size it to look like a flagpole. Place it behind all of our other `Game Play Layer` objects. Then place a `Flag` object from the `Effects` section of our **Asset Library**, and attach the flag image (in the `misc` folder). The result should look like the following screenshot:

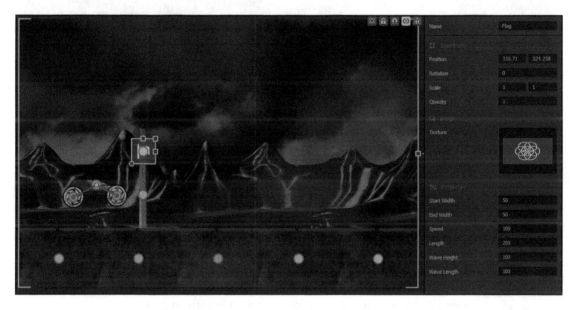

Now, do the same to your other two worlds, and try it out! If your flags are positioned a little oddly, just tweak the positioning, and retest! Now, let's really organize our scenes in each level…

Organizing your scenes

Whether you make your game progressive (using levels) or infinite (as with Ramblin' Rover), you're going to want some sort of order to your scenes. For instance, you wouldn't want the most difficult scene popping in right off the starting line. The players' psychology is simple: they want a challenge. It shouldn't be too easy, nor impossible to play. Remember, it should be challenging and fun…not work.

Let's start by opening up our `Mars Training Ground` world. Click on the ^ button in the bottom-right of the screen in the Scene Editor window. This turns the **Scene Editor** into the **Timeline Editor**. You should see something like this:

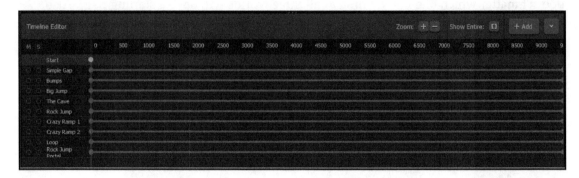

First, let's get this clear…*do not follow this next step*. I'm about to show you what it would look like (and how to do it) if we were to make this a level-based game. If we go to **Edit | Align Scenes**, this will make the scenes align so that as one scene ends, the next will begin. It will look like this:

The preceding screenshot shows how the scenes look when aligned. Seeing the text and numbers is not important. What is important is to show how all of the scenes align based on length so they start consecutively.

Basically, what this screen shows us is the distance at which *it's possible* to have a scene appear. So, since there is a distinct beginning and end to each scene coinciding with the ending of the previous scene and the beginning of the next…the only scene possible to play is the next.

Now, using this philosophy, adjust these by dragging the in points of the scenes so they overlap, as shown here:

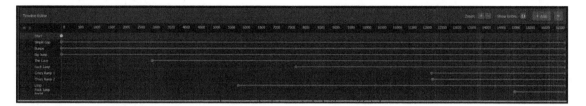

The image above shows the staggering we're going to do. Notice that the harder scenes show up as the player gets further into the game. The one exception is the loop level. This one comes in between **The Cave** and the **Rock Jump** levels.

So, using the philosophy we already stated, what we've done is make it so that only the harder levels show up as the player progresses throughout the game. Now, let's do the same with Gliese and Kepler. It's not exact. Just adjust the levels so they feel right to you. Here's what we came up with:

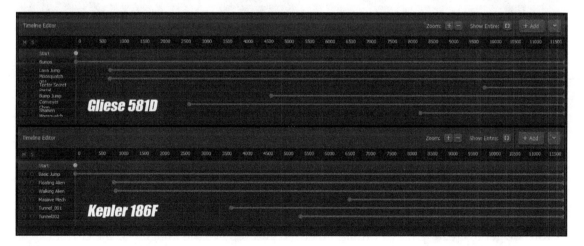

Menus and UIs

By now you should have a pretty good feel for how things work in Buildbox. The menu and UI editors work in *VERY* much the same way. However, we're going to be covering some aspects of Buildbox that we have not handled just yet. We'll be covering animations within Buildbox, text, and implementing controls.

Game Field UIs

When we created our secret level UIs on the Game Mind Map, they were placeholders until we got around to making our main Game Field UI. Now it's time to remedy this. First, we're going to finalize our main Game Field UI, then replace our secret level UIs with instances of our finalized Game Field UI. Let's get to it.

From the Game Mind Map, *double-click* on the main **Game Field UI**. You will be confronted with the following screenshot:

You may recognize this as the overlay that is on our worlds while we play in the Preview Mode. We're going to completely redo this interface. It's just not what we're after in our game. The first thing we want to do is move the **Game Over** Event Observer (on the top-left of our UI) off to the non-visible area. Event Observers are more commonly known to coders as event handlers. All these do is look for something to happen, and then the software makes something else happen. In this case, it sends us to the Game Over screen when the game is over. They also don't need to be in the visible area of the screen. So, let's get it out of the way…drag it off to the left.

Setting up controls

Before we get to creating new buttons, go ahead and replace the images for the current (forward, reverse, and pause) buttons, and move them. Your UI should match the following screenshot:

Now, let's add some new buttons to control our Jump and Shoot actions. In the **Characters** section of the Asset Library, drag two `CharacterButtons` onto our UI. Rename these Jump and Shoot. Then, we set their **Functions** to `Jump` and `Shoot` respectively. Drag our Jump and Shoot button graphics to the **Image** field, and make sure **Stick to Edge** is ticked. Your screen should look like the following screenshot. We've drawn a box around the fields we altered so you can find them easily.

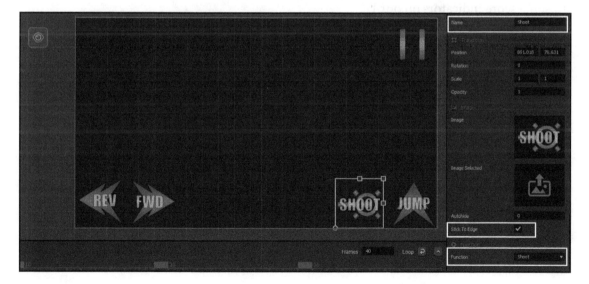

Just one more control to add! You may notice that there is no button control on our UI for our lean (doing flips). This one's actually pretty easy. We're going to add an accelerometer control. An accelerometer is a device inside mobiles, tablets, and some laptops that senses movement. This means that when they twist the device, it will affect the lean on the rover. Our game will now have a physical element to it, which will increase our fun factor.

Drag in an `Accelerometer` object from the **Characters** section of our Asset Library. You don't have to put this anywhere in the visible UI. We put ours just below the Game Over Event Observer. Just set the **Control Type** to **Rotate**, and the Sensitivity to `1.5`. That's it! By default, the Rotate control affects the lean. It should look like the following screenshot:

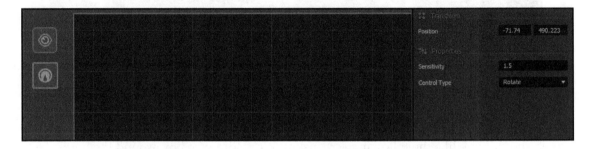

That's it; our game has all of the controls necessary to play on a mobile device. Now, let's set up some score indicators on our UI.

Dynamic text (score indicators)

Before we actually place any text on the UI, let's set up our Default Font. Just as we did before, open the **Font Editor**, and make the settings for the Default Font as shown in the following screenshot:

We're using the `Impact` font. Unfortunately, due to licensing we can neither provide this font, nor a link. However, nearly every free font website has some version of this font. Our **Font size** is 50, **Shadow Offset** is 3X3, and all options are ticked. Our gradient is yellow to brown, and the stroke color is black.

Now, we'll put in some static text (text that does not change) as labels. First, bring in a Default Font asset and place it on the screen. We'll rename this object Distance, and set the **Text** to read `Distance:`. Don't forget to tick **Stick To Edge**. This will help keep the object's position in relation to the edge of the device's screen. Remember, different devices have different resolutions on their screens. The result should look like the following screenshot:

Now, duplicate this object (using the S key). This one should be named, and read Coins. Now, you should have a UI like the following screenshot:

Ok, great! So we've got our static text and buttons, now let's make those values show up. Go ahead and duplicate the **Coins** text object (using the D key). For this copy, though, we're going to change the **Function** to Score. You'll see a few fields change based on this option. One of these is a new field called **World**. Set this to All. We could set this to show just the coins gathered in this try for the player, or just the coins gathered in this world. But we want a total count of coins so that the player knows if they have enough for that rover they've been saving up for. We also want to set the **Score Type** to Coins, and the **Amount** to Total in order to accomplish this goal. You should end up with something like the following screenshot:

Now, we'll do the same thing with **Distance** (with a few exceptions). For this dynamic text field, we'll still set the Function to Score. But we want to set our **World** field to `Current World`, our **Score Type** to `Distance`, and our **Amount** to `Current`. What this does is give us a current running total of our distance on this attempt in our current world. It should look like the following screenshot:

Now, back on the Game Mind Map, you should delete the secret world UIs and replace them with copies of this UI. It should look like the following screenshot:

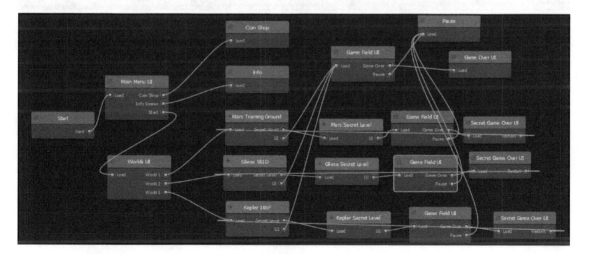

Game Over UIs

Just like our Game Field UIs, the Game Over UIs for the secret levels were mere placeholders. Let's go ahead and alter our master **Game Over UI** (double-click it to edit).

Let's start by setting up the background. Right now, that layer is named **Untitled**, and is a simple gray solid. Rename this layer BG, and replace the image with the one called GameOver2.png (located in the MenuAssets folder). It should look like the following screenshot:

Ok, before we go any further, use the same methods mentioned earlier to add a white font the same size as our Default Font (named White Regular), and another gold font (the same as our Default Font) that has a size of 100 (named Gold Large). They should look like this:

Fantastic! Now that we have some fonts ready for our game over screens, let's populate them. First, let's replace our Game Over text (which is currently an image) with actual text. Use the **Gold Large** label object we just created, and enter GAME OVER in the **User Text** field for it. Scale it a bit and position it so the object looks as shown in the following screenshot:

Now that we have *some* text on our Game Over UI, let's put some indicators on here to show our players how they did. Using our previous methods, let's add some text elements to our screen to match the following screenshot:

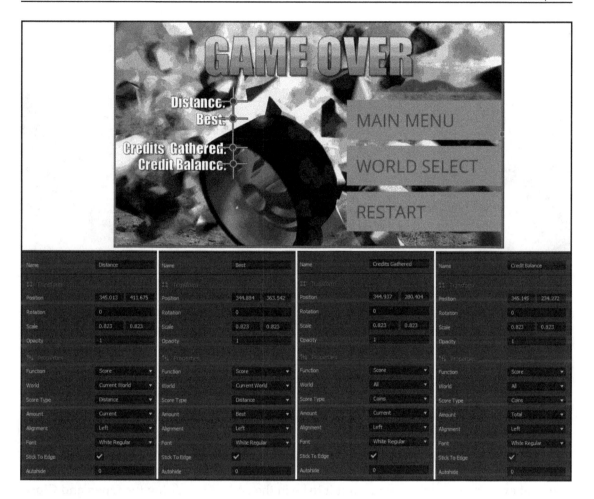

The preceding screenshot shows the locations of our text blocks, along with the properties of our corresponding dynamic text blocks. We use our *White Regular* font for these blocks.

Awesome! Now, to finish the static look of our Game Over screen (we'll get into why we called it that in a moment), just replace the graphics for our three buttons with the graphics shown here:

Great! So we've got our basic look for the Game Over screen. So, we mentioned before that at the bottom of these UIs is an animation timeline. Now, we're going to work with that…

How to animate a menu

The reason we work with the **Idle** part of the animation timeline first is because this is where everything lands and stays while waiting for user input. So, it's important to make sure that everything is where you want it to be in the end *before* editing the **Open** and **Close** animations.

Everything you do here is translated to the **Open** and **Close** animations *before* you edit those animations. However, if any changes are made to **Open** and **Close** and then you edit the **Idle**…the results can be a bit counter-productive.

Now that you're completely confused, let's explain what these **Open**, **Idle**, and **Close** animations are:

- **Open**: This is a brief animation that will play when the screen is loaded
- **Idle**: Idle is the state after the Open animation that will repeat until the user clicks on a button to take them to another UI or World
- **Close**: A Close animation will play after user input as a transition to the next UI/World

So, if you've ever authored a DVD, you're familiar with these types of transition screen. We're not going to bother with an Idle animation. If we were working with a cute game (like our basic template game with the eyeballs and shoes), we may consider an Idle animation with the character bouncing, or the sky passing by. For this game, any appropriate animations (like, say, a rover shooting or blowing up in the background) would be too resource-inefficient. So, let's just have our buttons and text slide in from the sides on open, and slide out on close. That brings us to the next section.

Computer animation 101

An animation (whether it's an image sequence, or an animation from within Buildbox) is essentially a sequence of still images known as frames. There are two types of frame: Keyframes and Tween-frames (also called keys and tweens). What are these two types really? Have a look:

- **Keyframe**: A keyframe is also called a pose. It's a frame where the animator sets an object in a specific position, rotation, or scale, then another keyframe in a different pose a second or two down the timeline. Then the rest of the frames would be filled in.
- **Tween**: This is all of the frames in be-*tween* the keyframes. The computer will fill these in to get from the user-defined keyframe to the next keyframe.

The following screenshot shows an example of a ball bouncing with three keyframes, and the rest of the frames filled in (with computer-generated tweens):

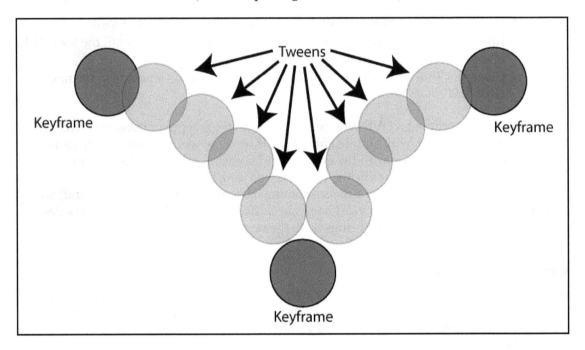

Whether you're developing the next great *Pixar* blockbuster feature film or creating animated menus in Buildbox, this is essentially how all computer animation works…keys and tweens.

Luckily (for us) the computer generates all of our tweens. But we do have an opportunity to tell it *how* to generate those tweens using motion curves. We'll get to those in a moment. For now, let's generate some keyframes, and get to animating our Game Over UI.

Animating the open

What we really have to remember is that the open scene is *before* the Idle scene, so we need to end up in the same position as the Idle scene to make it look good without hiccups in the motion. Let's start by clicking the **Open** button in the **Event** field inside the timeline window. We are now officially editing the Open scene.

Think of Frames in Buildbox in terms of the NTSC standard (around 30 frames per second). You can set how long the scene is by adjusting the **Frames** field. Let's go ahead and set that to 30 (or ~1 second). The orange block inside the timeline represents the current time marker (or where we're at within that 30 frames of opening animation). The line of gray hollow blocks is where we'll see keyframed (a white hollow block) or tween (gray hollow blocks) frames. For now, drag that orange block to the end of the timeline (or frame 30). The animation timeline window should look like this:

The first thing we should do is set a keyframe for an object at the end of the animation timeline to match where it should be at the beginning of the Idle animation. So, select the **Main Menu** button. Hit the Record button (the button with a white dot in it just left of the timeline) to turn keyframing mode on. In order to set a keyframe, just click inside the x-**Position** field in the properties window for the **Main Menu** object, and hit the *Enter* key on your keyboard; **do not actually change the value, just hit** *Enter*. The result should look like the following screenshot:

Notice that the last frame turned into a white hollow box. This means it is now a keyframe.

Now, move the orange block back to frame 20, and move the Main Menu object off-screen to the right. BAM! You just created another keyframe. Now the button will slide in from the right of the screen, and end up on the screen in about 1/3 of a second. But if you try it out (by hitting the Play button), you'll see that the motion is really...linear. It just kind of *chunks* in from the right, and we want smoother movement. What we really want is the appearance that the button is hitting the brakes and coming to a stop by continuously slowing down. This kind of movement is known as ease.

Remember how we talked about editing motion curves? Here's where that comes into play. If you click on the button marked with the ^ character in it on the right side of the animation timeline, you'll open the motion curve window. You'll notice some orange lines with orange circles at the end on each keyframe. You can grab these orange circles (called handles) to adjust your motion curve. Do this so that it looks like the following screenshot:

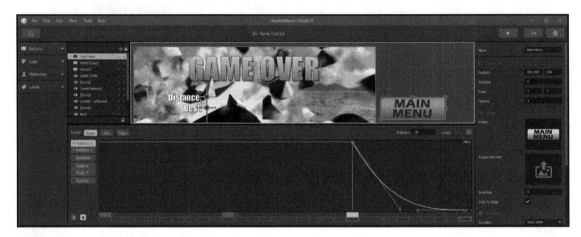

The vertical area of the graph represents the x-Position value, and the horizontal corresponds to time. So you can see that it moves drastically at first, and slows down to a stop at the end.

Let's show you one more button before we ask you to move on to doing the rest of the objects in the scene. Do the same thing with the **World Select** button. But with this one, let's stagger it back a bit in the timeline so it starts moving on frame 16, and ends on frame 25. The result should look like this:

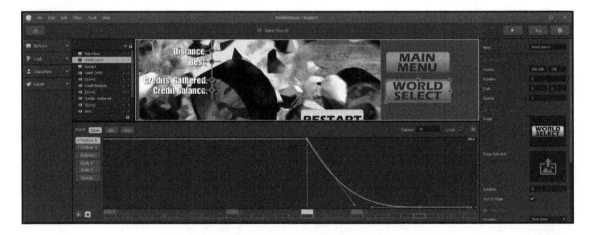

The idea is that if you don't have any of the objects coming on screen stopping at the same time, it becomes more organic and interesting to look at. Go ahead and do the same with all of the remaining objects (except the background) in the scene (including all of the text and dynamic text). Make sure none of them come in screen on the same frame. Remember, you can also use the Y-position in exactly the same way, and if things move from right to left (instead of left to right), the graph will appear inverted (starting low and ending high). The important part is that they start with a steep angle and end shallow.

Now that you're done with that, we can let the background fade-in by doing the same thing to opacity. Select the **BG** layer. Move the orange block to frame 30, click on the **Opacity** field, and hit your *Enter* key (to set an Opacity keyframe). Then, move the orange block back to frame 0, and change the **Opacity** value to 0. You should get a motion curve something like this:

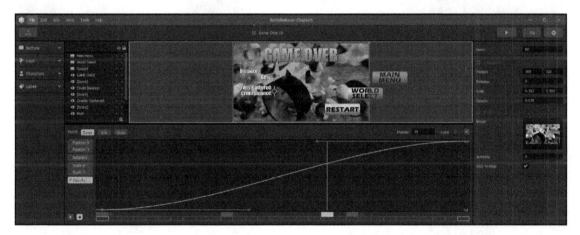

Sweet! You have your first animated menu. Now, we could create a Close animation as well. But our players are going to be in a hurry to get back into the game, so let's not do that. Go ahead and try out the game! It comes in in a cool way, but not so slow that players in a hurry to try again will be frustrated by it.

Now, as we did with the Game Field UI, duplicate the Game Over UI and replace the Secret Game Over UI objects with the copies. Don't forget to set the Restart button's function to Default (so you can link the restart behavior back to the main world it corresponds with). The final result should look like this:

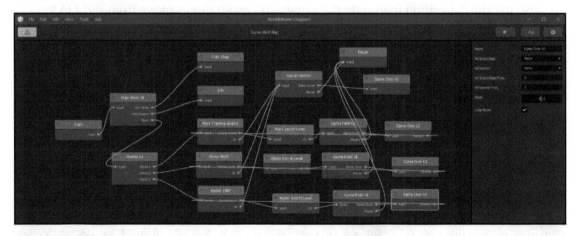

The Start UI (splash screen)

While the game is loading, the initial screen (which we are currently seeing as black) is the **Start** UI. All this UI is really for is to give the player something to look at, and possibly an indicator to see the loading progress. So because of the need to keep this screen resource-light and consider its narrow purpose, your options for placing objects on this screen are limited.

We're just going to add a company logo and a loading progress bar. Open up the Start UI, and drag the `LoadingScreen.png` file (inside `MenuAssets`) onto the stage as an **Image**. You'll notice that **Image** is the only option. This is due to the rudimentary nature of the Start UI. Then, drag a `Loading Bar` asset (in the **Preloader** section of the Asset Library) to the stage. That's it: **Loading** (Start) screen done! The result should look as shown in the following screenshot:

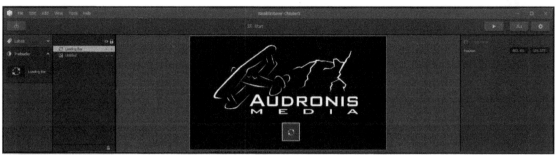

Let's move on to some more menus...

Main Menu and Worlds UIs

Let's start with the **Main Menu UI**. We're going to use the `MainBG.png` as the background image, and as another image (not a button) we'll use the `Rover001-MenuRender1.png` file. Both of these are in the `MenuAssets` directory. It should look like this:

You may be wondering why we used two different assets (rather than one image). Eventually, we'll animate the rover separately to make the appearance of this menu more interesting. We'll get there soon, but for now let's go ahead and replace our other buttons and position them. Also, let's create a copy of our **Gold Large** font, but with a font called Eras Bold ITC (and name it Title Font), and use that font to make the title of our game (replacing the Game object) so the UI looks like this:

So, what we've done here is simply replaced all of our buttons, and replaced the Game graphic object with text. Another benefit to having the Rover separated from Mars was that we were able to put it on top of all the other layers. We also added two bars (TitleStripe.png) above and below our title text to give it a slightly more interesting look. Finally, we put in a black box (Gray_Backer.png) that is semi-transparent behind out title block to help the text stand out a bit more.

Great! So we have an interesting Main Menu. Now, animate Open using the keyframing techniques we showed you. Be creative, and try keyframing different attributes like **Opacity**, **Scale**, and **Rotation**. If you're curious about what choices we made for our animations, feel free to open the RamblinRover-Chapter5 project to check out our **Main Menu**.

Let's move on to our **Worlds UI**. Now that you know how to build menus, we're going to speed up a bit. Try to create the UI so it looks like the following screenshot:

You may notice that we scaled the background image to get it positioned to see the spaceship a bit better behind all the buttons and text, and the addition of two more navigation buttons (one to select a rover before going to the game field, and one for instructions on how to play). Those navigation buttons have a `Default` **Function**, so we'll be able to hook them up to other UIs soon. Finally, we replaced the actual world selection buttons with graphics of the planets we'll be visiting (again, courtesy of NASA), and added supporting text using the fonts we've already created. Again, animate an Open animation for this screen...and we're done with it!

Character selection (Rover selection) UI

This is one of a few new UI screens we're going to have to create. So start off by creating a new UI (called Rover Selection) in the Game Mind Map and connect it to the **Worlds UI** as shown in the following screenshot:

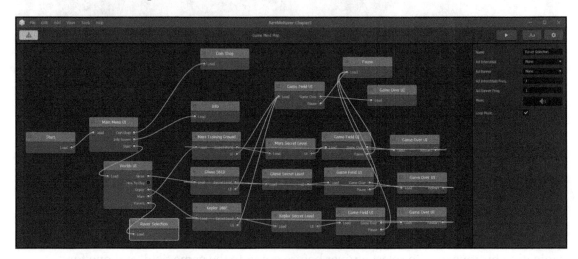

Now, just create a UI that looks like the following screenshot as a base:

Obviously, the **Function** on the Back button is `Back`, and the **Function** on the Store button is `Default`. You may wonder why we positioned it toward the top of the screen. This is because banner ads appear on the bottom section of the screen, and we intend to put banner ads on this UI. For most others we'll use a different type of ad, but we'll get to all of that later.

Buildbox has a great carrousel-style character selection button. Let's implement that now. Under the `Characters` section in the Asset Library, drag the `Multiple Unlock` object out to the scene in the center. Rename it Character Selection. Most of the parameters in here are self-explanatory, but let's go over the ones we changed. First, we set the **Label Vertical Spacing** to `-120`. This will set the text labels (derived from the character names) just below the characters. Positive numbers would put the label above. Furthermore, we want to set our **Label Name** to our `White Regular` font. Also, we set the **Spread** to `300`. This sets the distance between the *center* of each character to 300. Your results should look like this (once you resize the object to match):

We also added a credit balance using the same methods as on the Game Over screens (because the two upgraded rovers will cost in-game currency), and a call to action for them to buy more credits from the store.

The final step on this screen is to use the `Unlock.png` file as the **Unlock Button** for our Character Selection object.

Notice something funky here? The object is using the Default Animation for each character. So, it has no wheels. This would be fine if we were doing a game that didn't utilize wheels, but we want this to look better. For some reason, it will always display the first frame of the Default Animation in our editor, but when we compile or use preview mode (when we play the game), this object will use a Character Icon.

To fix this, we need icons for each character. To do this, we're going to need to go back to a world and open up characters' properties. Let's go do that.

For each character, you're going to need to use the **Add Component** button to add a `Character Icon`.

The first thing you're going to notice is that there are three new fields: **Regular Icon**, **Locked Icon**, and **Selected Icon**. Their purposes are exactly as they seem. In the `MenuAssets` directory, you'll find `Rover001-SelectionIcon.png`, `Rover002-SelectionIcon.png`, and `Rover003-SelectionIcon.png`. Use these for each rover as their **Regular Icons**. Similarly, use their `Locked` and `Selected` variants in the **Locked Icon** and **Selected Icon** fields. The training rover will be free, and therefore will never be locked (so we don't need a Locked Icon for this rover). The results should look like the following screenshot:

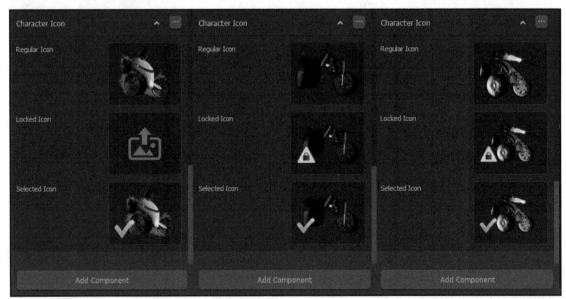

The preceding image shows the replaced icons on our three rovers. This must be done in a world (it doesn't matter which you chose). Our Mars Training Rover (left), our K.R.A.B.B. (middle), and our Phoenix (right) have all had their selection icons replaced.

Since we're already working on the properties of our rovers, let's quickly change their availability (so that they cost coins to purchase). To change this, just scroll up the Properties window until you come to a section called **Monetization**. Here, all we have to do is change the **Purchase Method** from Free to In Game Currency. Then we just set our price. Go ahead and change the K.R.A.B.B. to 10,000 and the Phoenix to 100,000. Now, let's finish up our menus...

Finishing up our Menu UIs

At first we wanted to keep our Game Mind Map as simple as possible. So, we left our Main Menu and World Select buttons alone with their Back **Functions**. But we're starting to get to the point where we may forget to turn those over to Default. Go ahead and jump into each of our Game Over UIs, and set those actions now. Then, connect them up. Your Game Mind Map should look like a spider web of complexity:

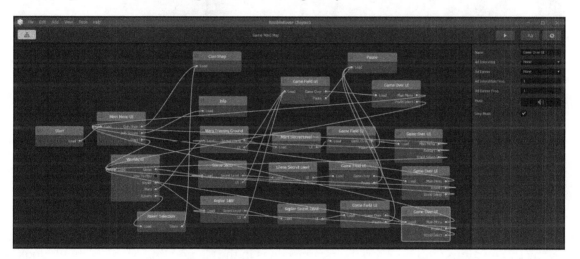

Let's knock the rest of these UIs out of the way.

The Info UI

This UI is pretty easy. This is where we put all the credits associated with the game, and the copyright information. We use the `TychoStarmap.png` file for the background. All of the rest is just text lines, with one exception. The book cover is a `URL Button` (with the URL set to where this book can be bought from the publisher's website). It looks like this:

Pause UI

When the game is paused, the game is still present…just paused. The pause UI is rather like an overlay. So, we'll replace the background with our `Gray_Backer.png` (semi-transparent block) image, and scale that image to fill the whole screen. Then, the player can still see the game in the background. The Game Field UI is replaced (so we don't have to worry about things getting too busy. Don't forget to reset the **Main Menu** and **World Select** buttons to `Default` **Functions** (and hook up their connections in the Game Mind Map). It should look like this:

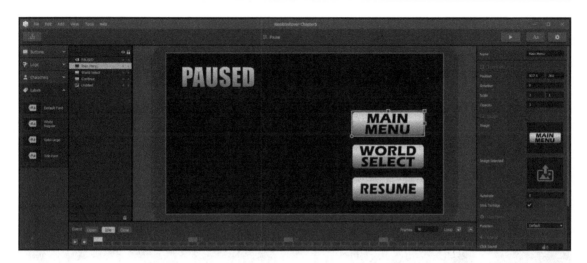

How to play UI

We still need to create this UI and connect it, so in the Game Mind Map, please create a new UI called *How To Play*, and connect it up to the How To Play output on the **Worlds UI** node. Now, we just need to create some instructions with a Back button (setting the **Function** of the button to Jump Back). We made our instructions to look like this:

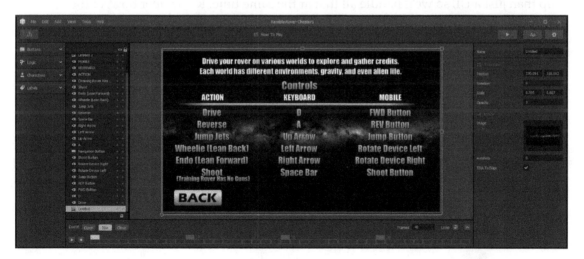

And thus, your final Game Mind Map should look like this:

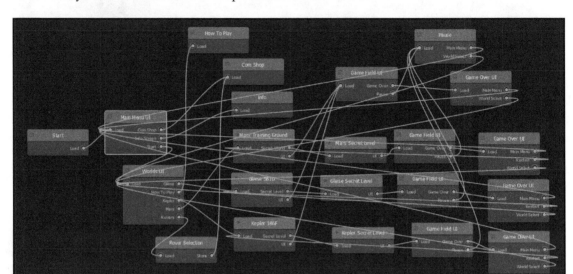

And that's it! All of our UIs are done! Or are they? In fact, we did not do our coin shop just yet. But as that relates a lot to monetization, we're going to save that for the next chapter (Chapter 6, *Monetization — Ramblin' Rover, Part 4*). There's a lot more to setting up a coin shop than just a UI, so we'll handle all that at the same time. Remember how, at the beginning of this book, we said that you'd understand complicated Game Mind Maps? Mission accomplished! Now, let's move into one of the easiest facets of Buildbox as a bit of a break from all the brain trauma we've incurred with this deluge of information and UIs.

Music and sound effects

Buildbox has made the implementation of music and sound effects super easy. It's a lot like replacing graphics on assets. You just drag your audio file (an MP3) onto the speaker icon in the properties field of whatever you'd like to assign it to. Let's get to it.

Adding a musical soundtrack to your game

There are lots of ways and philosophies for doing this. Each UI can have its own background music. It's important to know that with Buildbox, the music will keep playing until it is overridden by another piece of music. What does this mean? It means that if you set a piece of music to play, it will continue playing across all UIs unless another UI that pops up has its own music. For instance, menu music will continue to restart on each menu you go to (if each menu has music assigned). Also, if you assign music to a world...it will restart every time the player restarts the level.

This can get tiresome, and just downright annoying to a player. So what I do is create one MP3 file with several distinct pieces of music in it. I then assign that music to ONLY the Main Menu. Then, the user gets an uninterrupted string of music that repeats every ten minutes of gameplay...no matter what UI they go to (unless they revisit the initial Main Menu – which is rare).

Music is also extremely resource intensive (unless you want it to sound like someone passing gas in the soundtrack). So, by having only one MP3 file playing, we can lighten our resources a bit. But even this (by far) is the largest file of the whole game. It comes in at around 10 MB because it is a 128 Kb/s (kilo-bits per second) 48 KHz (48,000 samples per second) stereo file. It's the base quality for your standard broadcast FM radio station...so at least it'll sound decent.

We also mixed our music so that it's -9db. That means it's lower in volume from our sound effects by 9 decibels. We do this for two reasons: the sound effects in the game are more important than music because they let the player feel the game better, and because sound is additive, meaning that sounds piled all on top of each other can easily over-modulate (or overload) the audio and cause distortion.

Applying the music is a simple matter. You'll find the file `GeneralGameplay.mp3` in the `Sound/Music` folder of our content directory. On the Game Mind Map screen, just select (don't open) the `Main Menu UI`. Drag the music from your file browser onto the speaker icon next to the **Music** field in the **Properties** window. And here is the result:

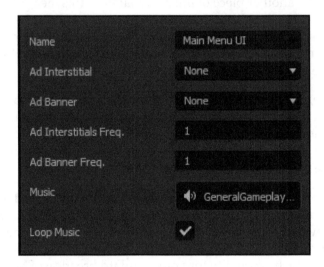

And there we have it. Our game has music. Now that you've (no doubt) played through the game several times...see what a difference just adding a music track can make. Play it with music! Our sound effects will take it to an even higher user experience level.

Adding sound effects

Adding sound effects is a very similar process to adding music. It's just a drag and drop proposition. The important thing to remember is that all of the MP3 sample rates and quality settings should be the same across all our files. Although Buildbox can play them all together (no matter their rate), some devices have issues with playing different formats at the same time. Remember, music is always playing in the background, and you'd hate to have a bug in your game where, as soon as a sound effect is played, the game crashes.

If you don't have the benefit of a complete sound studio, free sound effects can be found at various websites. We used `http://www.freesound.org` for some of ours, and generated the rest ourselves. But as with graphics, you can always use contractors from websites such as fiverr (`https://www.fiverr.com/`) for sound effects, or even custom music.

Also, sound effects are not assigned to objects at the world level...they're global. So, if we go into our Mars Training Ground and assign sound effects to our Mars Training Rover if someone uses the Mars Training Rover on Gliese...that same sound effect will apply. Basically, they're assigned by object...regardless of the World. Since we used this as an example, let's set up our Mars Training Rover.

Inside any world, just select the Training Rover from the Asset Library and in the **Properties** window, navigate to the **Sound** section. Now, just drag the `Explosion.mp3` file to the **Defeated Sound** field and the `AirJet.mp3` file to the **Jump Sound** field. Both of these files are in the `Sound/SFX` directory. And that's all that there is to it. Your results look like this:

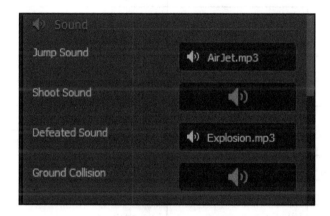

Great! Pretty simple, right? Unfortunately, there is no motor sound as of yet in Buildbox, but hopefully a future update will have this option. It'd be really cool to have our bigger rovers sound ominous, and the Training Rover sound like a Prius. No matter though, let's move on.

The following chart shows what sounds to assign to which parameters on objects in this game (starting with the object we just worked with). Go through each object and assign the sounds:

Object	Parameter	Sound file
Training Rover	Jump Sound	`AirJet.mp3`
	Defeated Sound	`RoverDeath.mp3`
K.R.A.B.B.	Jump Sound	`RocketJet.mp3`
	Shoot Sound	`LaserShot.mp3`

	Defeated Sound	`RoverDeath.mp3`
Phoenix	Jump Sound	`RocketJet.mp3`
	Shoot Sound	`MissileShot.mp3`
	Defeated Sound	`RoverDeath.mp3`
	Taking Damage Sound	`DamageExplosion.mp3`
Rock001	Death Sound	`Explosion.mp3`
Lava	Idle Sound	`Lava.mp3`
Moosquatch	Idle Sound	`Moosquatch.mp3`
	Death Sound	`MoosquatchDeath.mp3`
Moosquatch Shaman	Idle Sound	`MoosquatchShamen.mp3`
	Death Sound	`MoosquatchDeath.mp3`
Mech Walk	Idle Sound	`MechWalk.mp3`
	Death Sound	`Explosion.mp3`
	Taking Damage Sound	`DamageExplosion.mp3`
Psycholpse Shooting	Idle Sound	`Psychlopse.mp3`
	Death Sound	`PsychlopseDeath.mp3`
Laser Shot	Idle Sound	`LaserShot2.mp3`
	Death Sound	`DamageExplosion.mp3`
Psychlopse Walking	Idle Sound	`PsychlopseWalking.mp3`
	Death Sound	`PsychlopseDeath.mp3`
NormalCoins (Action)	Start Sound	`10Credits.mp3`
RedCoins (Action)	Start Sound	`100Credits.mp3`

And there it is! All of the sounds. The Laser Shot is a bit different. We used an idle sound with a long silence at the end in order to have a sound generated whenever an enemy fires their laser. Also, the **Taking Damage Sound** field is NOT in the **Sounds** area of the properties window. Instead, it is in the **Damage** area (because it is part of the Damage component).

Give your game a try with sound now! It's a much better experience for sure. If there are any sounds that are not to your taste, feel free to make sounds that are! Have some fun with it.

Summary

Well, we're finally there. Not there at the end, but in terms of having our actual gaming experience complete...we're there. We've learned about creating multiple characters in our games with their own attributes, weapons, and even their ability to take damage. We've also learned how to create menus, UIs, and even learned how to animate open and close scenes for those menus and UIs. And finally we learned how to implement sound into our game field.

Now we could get into sounds for each button click within our menus...but we're already pushing the limits with resources for mobile (with a computer game, this is more of a non-issue), so we're going to leave sounds on menus alone. But it works *exactly* the same way...just drag and drop sounds onto sound fields.

In the next chapter, we're going to learn about how to actually make money from our game. Of course, you could always charge for your game. But less people want to pay for games in the app store. The best way is through other monetization strategies, and we're going to learn all about that!

Take a break...play your game! And when you're ready to move on...we'll see you in the next chapter.

6

Monetization – Ramblin' Rover, Part 4

Making and playing your own video games is definitely fun. But what really sets the pros apart from the hobbyists? There are a lot of hobbyists out there with talent that rivals the highest echelons of the professional ranks. But by definition, the difference between a pro and a hobbyist is income...*money...moolah...da cabbage*.

Separating a customer from their money

In this day where there are a ton of great games out there at no cost with (previously said) amazing hobbyist developers, how can you get a customer to pay you money for an experience they may get for free? It comes down to a few basic philosophies.

Free game, or paid game?

This is probably the toughest way to make money...by actually charging for the game itself. If you're coming straight out of the gate with your first game... this is not really an advisable way to go. There are exceptions to that rule (for instance, you feel sooo strongly that you have a ground-breaking new game that *everyone* will want to play). But in general, customers will avoid games from indie developers that cost money. So IF you ever do a paid game... you may want to make a *light* version of it as a demo that people can play to bait the hook for a paid game.

To have ads, or not to have ads?

Ads are a pretty good way to earn some money, especially if your game is free. We'll be using this model in Ramblin' Rover. You really have to be careful with this model, though. It's far too easy to go overboard and annoy your players to the point of no longer wanting to play your game (and possibly give you a bad rating – which will pretty much kill your game distribution). Ads come from third-party providers, but are placed within the Buildbox interface with just a few clicks. Some ads are paid by click, and some by impression, and others are a balance of both. Don't know what any of that means? Don't worry… we'll get into it in just a moment.

Coin store

As you know, we set up our two upgraded rovers so that they cost in-game currency. There's two ways to acquire these *coins*. Obviously, one way is picking up the ones we placed in the game. But, players could also choose to purchase coins with real money to get rovers without *grinding* in the game. Other perks can also be purchased through this store (including unlocking potential maps, and even turning off advertising for a fee)!

Implementing advertising

The actual implementing of advertising in Buildbox is a relatively simple proposition. It's a three-step process:

1. Sign up with a provider.
2. Link to your account in Buildbox.
3. Enable ads in UI properties.

Ok… so each of those steps has several sub-steps. But in reality, everything about this is pretty easy. If you can order goods on the Internet… you can do this. Let's get started.

Signing up with a provider

First off, you're going to need to choose providers (or a provider) for ad services. Each platform has its own requirements on what it allows through Buildbox to provide ads for. The following chart shows the providers on the various platforms:

Apple iOS	Apple Mac App	Google Play	Amazon App	Windows
Chartboost		Chartboost	Chartboost	
RevMob		RevMob	RevMob	
AppLovin		AppLovin	AppLovin	
LeadBolt		LeadBolt		
AdMob		AdMob		
HeyZap		HeyZap		
Facebook		Facebook		
				Vungle

The first thing you'll notice is that the Mac App Store doesn't have any ad connectivity with Buildbox. Windows Store has only one provider that no others work with. Also, Steam doesn't even have an option for advertisements.

You don't need to use every provider for placing ads. This just gives you better options for what you may or may not want to use. We're going to use RevMob for Ramblin' Rover (as it's one of the most compatible, and therefore requires minimal work), as well as Vungle (because it's the only one that works for the Windows Store). Don't worry though. Almost every service works the same way, and it's pretty much as simple as signing up on Facebook.

Let's start with RevMob (http://www.revmobileadnetwork.com). Once you sign up for an account and log in, you'll see this bar at the bottom of your web browser:

| Reports | Add iOS App | Add Android App | Add Amazon App | Add Mobile Website |

The middle three buttons are the ones we're concerned with (iOS, Android (Google), and Amazon Apps). If you click the **Add Amazon App** button, you're brought to the following interface:

Just enter `Ramblin Rover` in the **Media Name** field and submit. You'll then be confronted with this message:

Don't worry about the **Software Developer Kit** (**SDK**) part of the message. One of the beauties of Buildbox is that they've already integrated the SDK for all their supported ad providers!

Go ahead and do the same thing for iPhone and Android (as known as. Google Play). Your screen (when complete) should look like the following screenshot. There are a couple of exceptions. We set two of the statuses to *Live* to show you what it looks like, and we named our apps by the store name to show you that we've added all three. Yours should all be in *Testing* mode, and all should be titled *Ramblin Rover*.

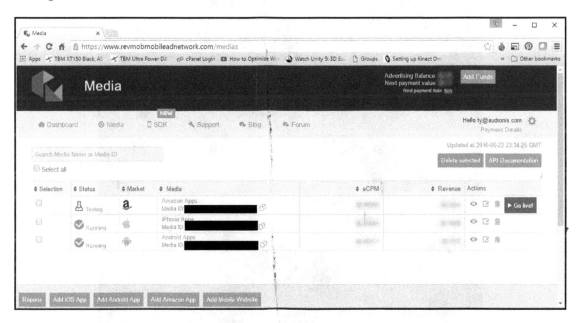

The Media IDs for your various distribution channels (redacted with black bars – these are private, and you should guard your Media IDs) will be important in a moment. Leave this browser window open, and open your Ramblin' Rover project in Buildbox.

Linking Buildbox to a provider

Open the Project Settings window (the gear icon in the upper-right of Buildbox), and select the **Advertisements** tab at the top. You should see this:

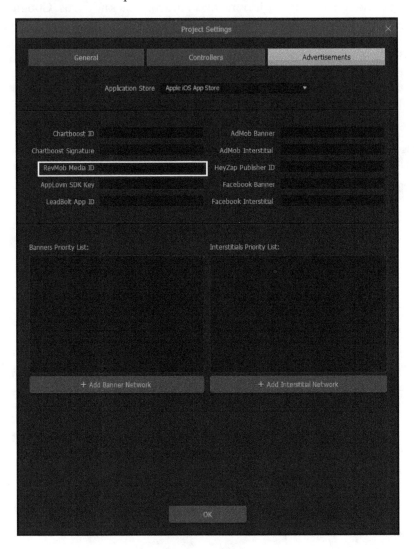

We've highlighted where we put the **RevMob Media ID** that we setup. Just select each (the **Apple iOS**, **Google Play**, and **Amazon App Stores**) from the **Application Store** drop-down menu, and copy the appropriate Media IDs into these **RevMob ID** fields (the field is unique for each dropdown).

Great! Now our ads are linked... but they can't be displayed yet. We now need to set a priority for both banners and interstitials. Select the **+ Add Banner Network**, and add RevMob to both banners and interstitials (for each of our three stores). It should look like this:

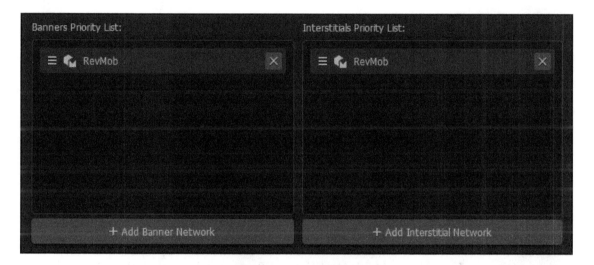

 Before we move on though... go ahead and sign up on Vungle (http://www.vungle.com) and do the same with our Windows Store. It should be noted that you should leave the Priority Lists blank for Windows Store. After talking to Buildbox Support... Vungle is the only service offered for Windows Store. So, the priority lists have been turned off. By the time you read this, they may have eliminated these Priority Lists from the Windows Store interface (due to the confusion), but just in case they're still there for you... we thought we should say something.

OK... so now we have the capability of displaying ads. But now we need to tell Buildbox *where* to put them. Close the **Project Settings** window, and let's do this.

What are banners and interstitials?

Banner ads in Buildbox are still image ads that are clickable links that appear on the lower-section of the screen (in broadcast TV… it's called a lower-third – the same area a newscast may put someone's name). So you have to be careful on what UIs you put these types of ads on. You don't want to block off buttons (or even worse… crucial game fields).

Interstitial ads are ads that are placed full-screen for a short time (or have a *close* button at the top-right). They pop up between UIs, and can be still images, or full-motion video.

With both of these types of ads, we need to be careful. We actually want to annoy our players… *but only ever so slightly*. This way, they're motivated to buy the *ad-free* version, but not so irritated that they give us a negative review, or stop playing.

Another good strategy is to have ads pop up only intermittently. For instance, a screen where a player is used to hitting *start over* several times… they *may accidentally* click on an ad (generating revenue). On the game over screen. So a *game-over* screen should have an interstitial pop up… but only every five-or-so times. Granted… this sounds a bit sneaky, but this is an actual strategy that game companies use to help with profits. Remember… if you want to be a professional, you need to take into account your bottom line.

Assigning ads to UIs

Let's start by selecting our main **Game Over UI**. You'll notice in the properties window that there are four ad-related fields (**Ad Interstitial, Ad Banner, Ad Interstitials Freq.**, and **Ad Banner Freq.**). This is where you set what ad provider to use, and how often it pops up.

The frequency number is based on how many times the UI appears before an ad pops up. So, if we set the **Ad Interstitial Freq.** to 5 and **Ad Interstitial** to RevMob; a RevMob video will pop up one out of every five game over screens. Go ahead and do that now. It should look like the following:

And yes… it really is *that* easy. Now just do the same thing with the rest of your Game Over UIs. You may be wondering right now, *wait a minute… what about Vungle?* We'll get to that later. For now, let's add a banner (as well as an interstitial) to the store page. Why not? Let's give them a reminder of why they should pay to remove all ads. Go ahead and add `RevMob` to both the **Ad Interstitial** and **Ad Banner** fields for our Coin Shop. Also, leave the frequencies at 1. This will make an interstitial and a banner appear every time this screen comes up. It should look like this:

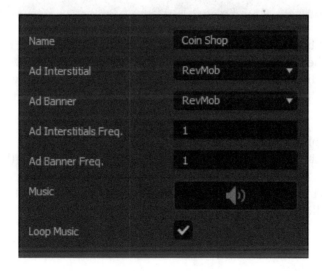

Now just do the same to the **Rover Selection UI**, and there you have it… our ads are complete! Once you have ad providers, implementing them in Buildbox is *extremely* easy. No code snippets, no SDKs… just plug in the account codes, and tell Buildbox where and how often you want ads. Now, let's get to that coin shop.

Building a coin shop (part 1)

This is almost as easy as setting up ads. Just a few minor complications. First, set up your **Coin Shop UI** to look like this:

The actual purchase buttons are made using the **Purchase Button** asset found in the **Buttons** section of the Asset Library. Before we can set these up, however, we must set up an action for the credit purchases to be linked to. And we mean literally an action on a game field screen. It doesn't matter which game field you go to, but we used the mars training ground.

Just drag in any graphic asset as an action. We used the Pause button graphic (so that we could easily tell what it was. Now that it's on the game field… delete it (by selecting it on the stage, and hitting the Delete key on your keyboard). Why? Because we want the action to exist, but we don't want it to be available during game play… only through a purchase. Set it up with the following settings:

Now set up another one (we used the forward icon for the graphic) called
HundredThousand with 100,000 **Reward Coins**. You may wonder why we used button
graphics, and not a new unique graphic. First, as the actions are never displayed, there is no
reason to make a new graphic. And second, reusing previously used graphics gives us the
possibility that in the final compilation, there will be no additional resource cost (as it's
another instance of the same graphic file). Let's go back to the **Coin Shop UI**.

Now, let's link up our credit purchase buttons to the actions in our game fields. Select the purchase button for the 10,000 credits, and make sure the settings look like the ones shown in the following screenshot:

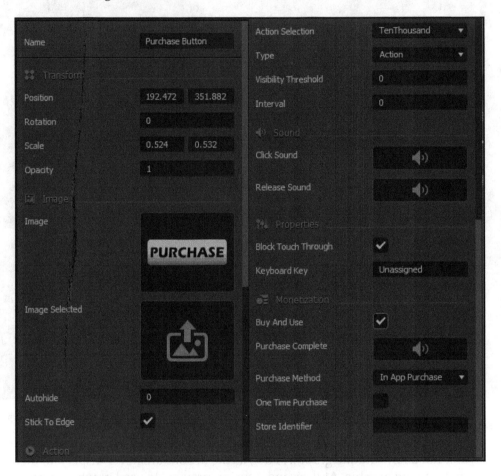

So, what we did here is select our TenThousand action from the game field in the **Action Selection** field. This links the reward. We also ticked our **Buy and Use** button (because we want the credits to go into their balance immediately). And finally, we selected **In App Purchase** from the **Purchase Method** drop-down menu. This all basically sets up everything we need to link this button to activate our action for a price. There's one more thing we'll have to do with this button (the **Store Identifier** field), but we're going to save that until we explain app IDs, and setting up your accounts for distribution channels. Leave this blank for now.

Do the same for the purchase button related to the 100,000 credit purchase (of course, linking it to the other action we created), and let's move on to our purchase button for removing ads.

Your settings for this button should look like the following screenshot:

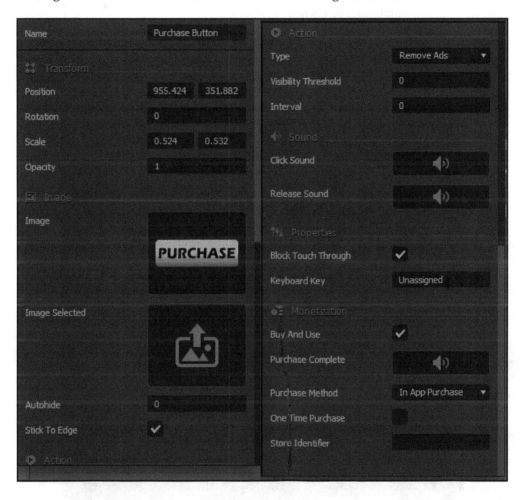

Adding video rewards

Video rewards are a great way to make money while not making your users pay for a single thing! Well, at least not with cash. Instead, they watch an advertisement and in turn, both you (the developer), and your player get a reward. You get paid, and your players get free coin rewards just for watching. Here's how it's done.

The first thing you'll need to do is go sign up for an account at HeyZap (`http://www.heyzap.com`). Once you sign up, just copy your publisher ID from your HeyZap account and put it in the Project Settings interface (for both your Google Play and iOS advertisements), as follows:

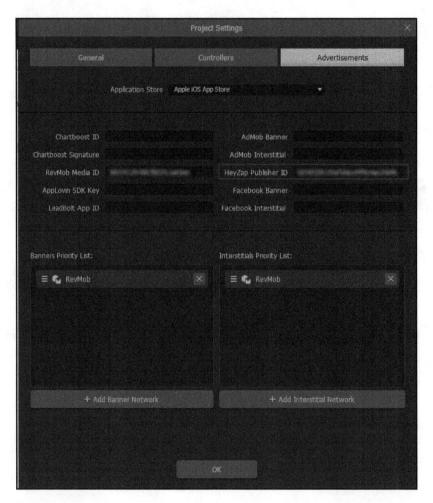

Now it's just a matter of setting up the button for the reward videos. Just like we set up the actions for our `10,000` and `100,000` coin buttons, you'll need to set up another action for the actual reward the player gets for watching videos. The bonus with this is that it completely bypasses the necessary entries in our distribution channels (which we'll cover in the next chapter) to buy items that we're selling. Instead, this is a simple transaction to watch an ad, so it's easy and quick to set up!

First, we replaced the *Purchase* graphic of our purchase button with one that reads *Watch Video*. This way the player knows they aren't buying anything. Then, (as we did with the other buttons), set the **Action Selection** to the one you just created to reward the player for watching the video. Once they've finished watching, they'll receive this reward instantly. Finally, in the Buy and Use section of the properties window, just set the **Purchase Method** to `Reward Videos` and the **Ad Network** to `HeyZap`. That's all there is to it! It should look like the following screenshot:

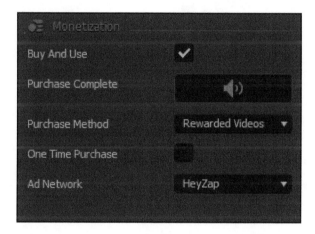

And there you have it! Our coin store is (mostly) complete. Only one more field to fill out for each purchase button as well as setting up our restore purchases button, and we'll handle that in just a bit.

Summary

We've learned some strategies for different monetization models, and discovered how to implement some of those strategies into our game. We've also learned about ad providers, and how simply we can implement those ads into a game to start earning some cash. Finally, we set up a coin shop where users can buy enough coins to buy our various rovers, as well as how to remove ads. Removing ads is a great strategy, because this gives a player an option to pay for the game, and see instant results from their expenditure (rather than having a free game with ads, and a paid game with no ads).

Get ready, because the next chapter will be packed with information. We'll be exporting our game for various distribution channels, compiling it into useable programs to be played on various platforms, and finalizing our coin shop!

7
Exporting and Compiling for Various Platforms – Ramblin' Rover, Finale

Possibly the biggest point of confusion with making an executable game with Buildbox is the difference between exporting and compiling. In general, when we're talking about exporting from Buildbox, we mean that Buildbox generates the projects needed for the **Integrated Development Environment (IDE)** for that platform (that is, Eclipse for Android, or xCode for Apple) to compile an executable code (the final program that runs on the platform). There are a few exceptions (Windows EXE and Steam needs compiling), where the final product is created from inside Buildbox.

If your brain just exploded, don't worry… by the end of this chapter, you'll understand exactly what all of this means.

Although Ramblin' Rover is conditionally (please check the EULA section) open source if you own this book; as there is already a Ramblin' Rover game on all of the app stores, you should not attempt to *actually* upload this game. You'll receive a lot of errors having to do with copyrights (and cause a lot of confusion in app stores, and possibly get inadvertently banned – as some app stores are more restrictive than others). What we present here is an example of exactly *how* it was uploaded to the app stores to educate you on how you can upload your own games.

Now that the obvious is out of the way…before we get started, there are a couple of things we need to do in order to prepare for export…

Optimizing game assets

Remember, we want our game to be as resource-light as possible. Not only does this ensure that it'll run on most devices, but it makes our game run as fast as possible (in the hope to avoid any hiccups due to older devices). In the quest to make our game, it's virtually assured that we have a lot of duplicated graphics, some graphics that are no longer even used, and the same goes for our audio. Let's get started by opening up our game in Buildbox.

Let's also save a new copy of the game once it's opened. I'm always weary of automatic optimization processes (as it's entirely possible to have the software accidentally remove required graphics or audio). So, by saving a *backup* of the game, we know that we can always go back without painstakingly restoring assets.

Under the **Tools** menu (at the top of the interface), systematically go down and run every remove process offered:

- **Remove Unused Level Objects**
- **Remove Unused Image Objects**
- **Remove Unused Sound Objects**
- **Remove Unused Scenes**
- **Remove Unused Components**

Some of these may read as **0 Objects Removed**, but you may be surprised with how many unused objects are removed from others.

Now we have to work with the Atlases. From the **Edit** menu, select **Atlases**. Buildbox works with large images that are broken up into a grid with each of our image files placed on those large images. This makes it easy for our game to quickly access a particular image (as it minimizes the number of files the program has to request). In the end, instead of referencing hundreds of image files, the game just grabs an Atlas, and shows one quadrant of it.

The problem is that if we have a ton of duplicated, or unused images, then the Atlas count can go up, and so does the overall size of the game. The following screenshot shows what the Atlas interface looks like:

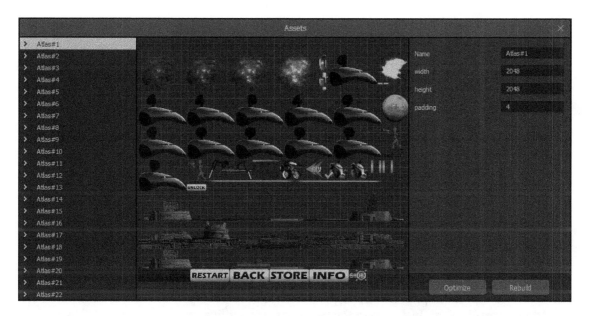

As you can see, even our image sequences (such as our explosion animation, or our animation of the Rover's satellite dish rotating) have each individual frame as an entry on the Atlas. This is one of the reasons that we carefully consider the size of our images when we make them. We don't want a section of the Atlas to be bigger than necessary. Bigger images means bigger Atlases, which means less efficiency. We can also see why we're limited to background images no larger than 2,040 in either dimension. 2,048 is the dimension of our Atlas, and there are 4 pixels of padding on each side (8 pixels total... 2048-8=2040).

Optimizing is easy. Just click **Optimize**, wait for it (unfortunately, there is no progress bar to let you know how close it is, but there is a message to let you know it is completed), then click **Rebuild**.

And that's it! We're all optimized and ready to begin the process of exporting… almost.

Signing up for distribution

Before we finalize the settings in our game (the build ID, leaderboard IDs, and store IDs) we need to set up our actual distribution channels. Distribution is probably what most of you bought this book to figure out. It's a murky process, and requires a great deal of patience and tenacity to finish. The sooner we start, the better though… right?

Google Play (Android part 1)

Start by going to the Developer Console (`https://play.google.com/apps/publish/signup/`). Signing up is an easy process. Just agree to the terms, and pay $25 per year to be a Google Play developer. That's really it! Now, let's set up our app. In the top-right corner of the Developer Console is a button called **+ Add new application**. Just type in the name for our application, and submit it. Then, choose to manage the application (not to upload an APK file). We're not going to actually manage the game (yet) though. On the left side of the screen, click **Game Services** and again, **+Add new application**.

Google Play game services are important for saved games, leaderboards, and other services the user takes for granted. Again, we need to add Ramblin' Rover for this. The interface looks like the following:

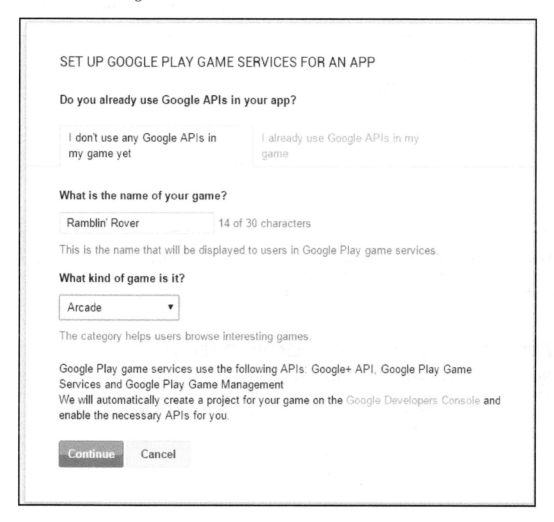

Go ahead and **Continue**. We'll circle back to the game details later. First, what we're trying to do here is make sure all of the frameworks are in place to set up our leaderboards within Buildbox. On the left side, click on **Leaderboards**. Now, select Add new leaderboard and name it `Best Rover Drivers` (then save it). You should now have something like this:

You'll be given an ID (in the screenshot it's been redacted with a black box). Copy this, or write it down. We'll need it later. We'll also come back and populate the rest of our fields in a bit… we just need this ID before we can export. Let's move on to Amazon.

Amazon App Store (Android part 2)

Now go to the Amazon App Store console (`https://developer.amazon.com/home.html`) and sign up for a new account. This one is free! Once you've signed up and confirmed your account, go to **Apps & Services** on the console, and select **Add a New App**. Fill out the form, as shown in the following screenshot:

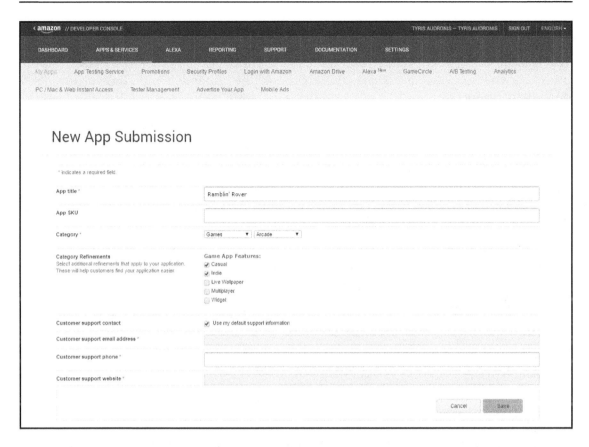

Now click **Save**. You'll see the following interface. Make note of the **Version ID** and **Application Key** (or also called API key). Both are shown as redacted in this screenshot:

Apple (iOS and Mac – iTunes)

This is by far the most convoluted and confusing of the developer programs. In fact, this process is what spawned the idea to write this book (the response to my YouTube tutorial on the export process).

First off, you must sign up for the Apple Developer Program (http://developer.apple.com). It's a pretty steep subscription price of $99 USD per year. But, it's one of the largest distribution channels around. So, what are you going to do?

Now, under your account, on the left-side, you'll need to click on **Certificates, IDs & Profiles**. Once on this screen, click on the + icon (top-right) and create both distribution and development certificates. Your iOS Certificates page should look like this:

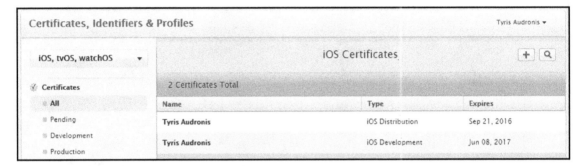

Not only do you need to sign up for the Developer Program, but you must now sign up for an iTunes Connect account (http://itunesconnect.apple.com). This one's free, but be prepared... there is a lot of paperwork associated with this (agreeing to policies and whatnot). You're also going to want to log in regularly to this account (after its created) because there is a constant need to agree to changes in these policies. Apple sure doesn't make it easy to make apps. Once you're all signed up, you'll get to this interface:

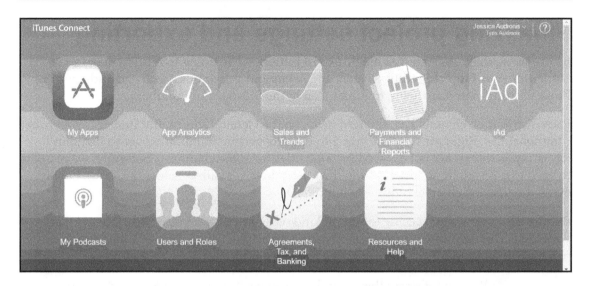

Ok… let's just let our Apple stuff sit for a while. There's more we need to do (because XCode and iTunesConnect are interlinked). We'll have to go through **several** steps when we get to exporting for Apple. We'll actually have to export it, then set it up on iTunesConnect, and then export it again for leaderboards. Yeah… thanks Apple. We have our accounts. That's enough for now. We have A LOT left to do for Apple, but we have our basic accounts set up.

Windows store and Steam

Windows store and Steam are completely separate exports, so we'll actually handle all the groundwork for leaderboards later. For now, just sign up for Windows Store (`https://dev eloper.microsoft.com/en-us/windows/programs/join`) which is $19.

Steam requires a bit of explanation. Steam has a program called *Steam Greenlight* (which you must sign up for as an indie developer). Submitting to Greenlight does *NOT* guarantee you a spot on the Steam store. Greenlight gives people a chance to see some screenshots and read a description of your game (but not even try it out), and if people like it… only then will Steam put it up for distribution. The cost is $100 to sign up. That's not $100 per year… just $100 period. All proceeds go to Penny Arcade's Child's Play charity (not Valve), so at least it's a good cause. But this lack of a guarantee of distribution has been likened by some to a $100 lottery ticket. It's highly controversial in the gaming community as the big boys can bypass this and still put their games on the store. You also must sign up through the Steam application (just search for Greenlight).

Finalizing project settings and exporting

Before we actually click on that magic export button, we're going to need to make a few entries into our **Project Settings** screen, and set up our purchases. Go ahead and open the Project Settings interface (using the gear icon in the top-right of Buildbox).

Each distribution channel has different fields on the General screen. But first, let's cover the commonalities. Right away, we're going to have to rename Ramblin' Rover to Ramblin Rover (apostrophes are not allowed in game titles for some channels). Secondly, we're going to need to place our icon (drag it from the Misc folder; it's called `Icon1024.png`). Finally, every distribution channel requires a Bundle ID.

Bundle IDs have a very specific format. It kind of looks like a reverse URL. Always start with `com`. Then comes your name or company name (we use `Audronis`), then the game name. So, it looks like `com.audronis.rover` in the end.

We cannot stress this enough... no special characters (&, @, and so on), and *NO SPACES*. Keep all these commonalities in mind as we move onto each platform's exports.

Let's just rip the band-aid off (so to speak) and get the hardest one over with first...

Exporting and compiling for Apple iOS

Ok... buckle up; this is the complicated one. First, it has to be said... you MUST have a Mac to run xCode. Technically, any *Hackintosh* (running MacOS on non-Apple hardware) is a violation of Apple's EULA (End User License Agreement). So it's not advisable. And if they ever find out, it can result in not only your app being removed from iTunes... but your user account being banned. Thanks Apple. I'm not aware of this ever actually happening. However, the spectre looms, so we advise you to consider this possibility.

We didn't bother with setting up the app in iTunes Connect because xCode needs to open something for the build ID to be known to iTunes connect. Don't worry; we'll set up xCode soon. First, let's just get our game exported.

Go ahead and set up the Project Settings interface to look like the following screenshot:

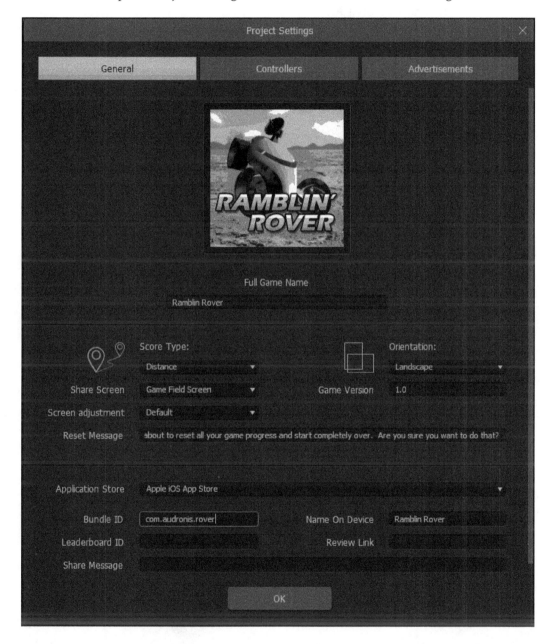

Notice we've used `com.audronis.rover` for our **Bundle ID**. For now, we have to leave our **Leaderboard ID** and **Review Link** blank. Thanks Apple. You may read that phrase a lot in this chapter. This process is relatively frustrating when compared to Google or Amazon. Go ahead and close the Project Settings window, and let's export this thing!

Go to **File** | **Export** | **iOS** and select an area to send your export to. It takes a bit, so if your Buildbox appears to *lock up*, don't worry… it's just exporting (there is no progress bar). That's it for Buildbox's end at this point. Now we need to compile using xCode on a Mac.

Don't worry; you don't have to invest in a $2500 Mac Pro. This can be done on a Mac Mini (which you should be able to get on eBay for just a couple hundred dollars). Power isn't necessary for compiling. We're using a 2008 Mac Mini, without so much as a keyboard or mouse. We're just using TeamViewer to access it from our Windows machine. You'll need to get the files from your Windows machine (if you're using Windows) to the Mac (thumb drive, network, Dropbox, and so on). We used a shared drive from our Windows machine to access the files from our Mac across the network. Just don't compile across the network (copy the files to the Mac… way too slow on a network).

Finalizing your dev settings on your Mac and iTunes Connect

First, you're going to need to download xCode from the App store (it's free). You may need to update your OS to do so. Next, back at the Apple Developer Console (the area where you can view your profiles and certificates). Click on each of your certificates, and download them to your Mac, as follows:

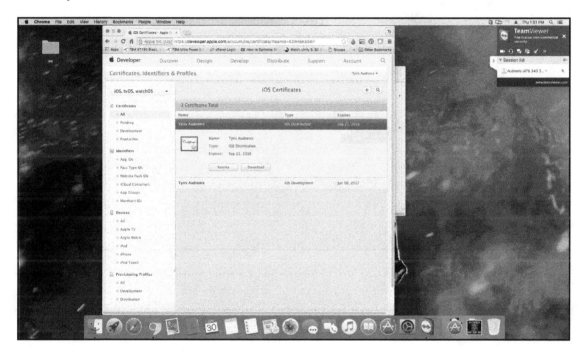

After they're downloaded, double-click each of them, and add them to your **Keychain Access**. You can double-check your Keychain to make sure they're in there by opening **Keychain Access** (if you don't know where it is, use the *Spotlight Search* feature on your Mac to find it). It should look like the following screenshot when the certificates are installed:

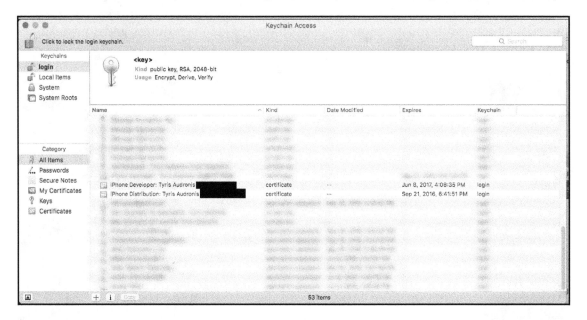

Now, inside the folder containing your Buildbox export, you'll find **PTPlayer.xcodeproj**. Don't worry that it's not called *Ramblin Rover*. For some reason, everything that comes out of Buildbox is called **PTPlayer**. It has literally *ZERO* effect on the final application name on the device. Double-click this file once xCode is installed (as shown in the following screenshot):

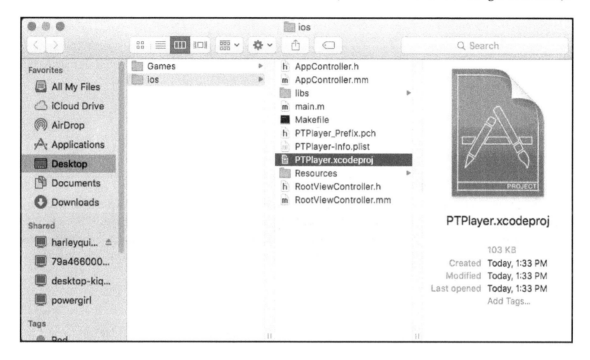

Now that we've got the project opened inside xCode, click on the **PTPlayer** listing on the left side of xCode. You'll see the project open up, and set the Team entry to you (your iTunes account), as follows:

Ok, now, to let iTunes Connect know that this project exists, we need to build it in a fashion (even though our project isn't complete and ready… we need to execute a build). So we're going to run a test (which builds it for an i-device simulator here on the Mac). From the top-menu, select **Product | Run**. Now just wait a beat or two (or many more), and an iPhone simulator is started and boots up (with the familiar Apple logo, the home screen, and then Ramblin' Rover starts up). You can surely test and play your game here, or just close the simulator. Your build has been done. Let's move on to iTunes Connect.

Log in to your iTunes Connect account on your web browser (doesn't matter if you use a Mac or PC at this point), and click on **My Apps**. At the top-left of the screen, you'll see a + icon (add new app). Fill out the form so that it looks like the following screenshot:

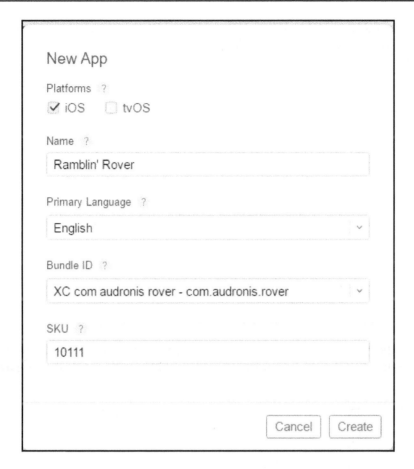

See how there is a Bundle ID all ready for you (that reads **XC com.audronis.rover –
com.audronis.rover**)? This is why we did an initial build of our game. When we ran our
test, a build (compile) was created, and xCode told iTunes Connect that you're working on
an app with that Build ID. Pretty cool if you're doing all your development using xCode…
kind of a pain in the badonkadonk if you're using anything else (Unity, Buildbox, and so
on). Shall we say it? Thanks Apple. Also, we just made up a number for the SKU. Ok…
moving on.

Before we can create our final build of our game, we need to get our leaderboard ID. So, at the top, select **Features**, and then on the left, select **Game Center**. You should have a screen like the following:

If you click on the little + icon to the right of **Leaderboards**, we can create a new leaderboard. Select **Single Leaderboard** as the type. Fill out the top half of the form as follows:

Notice that we used the same format as our Build ID for the **Leaderboard ID**. You don't *have* to do it this way. But it is easier to remember. For the **Localization** section, click on **Add Language**, and fill out the form as follows:

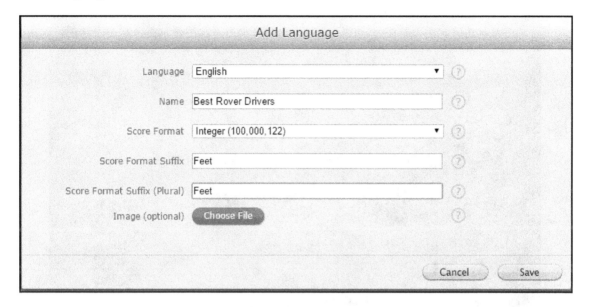

Go ahead and click **Save**, and then click **Save** again to save your leaderboard. Copy the **Leaderboard ID**, and go back to Buildbox, and place it in the **Leaderboard ID** field of your **Project Settings** window for iOS, as shown in the following screenshot:

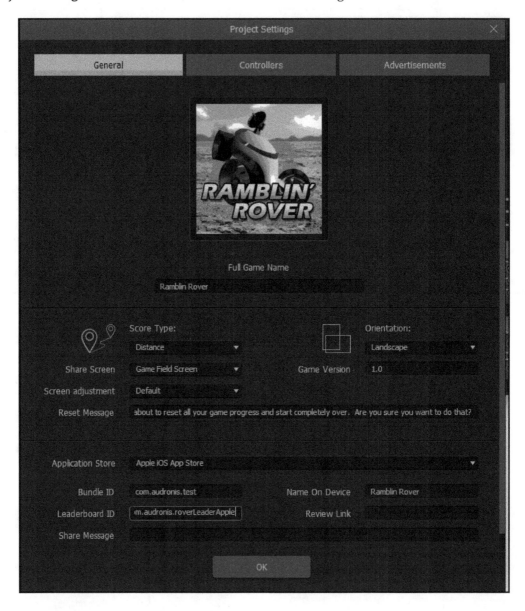

Now we need a review link (which is also our entry on the iTunes app store). The format is `https://itunes.apple.com/app/id####` (where the `####` is our app ID). If you click on the **App Store** entry at the top of the iTunes Connect page, under **App Information**, you'll find the **App ID**. As our **App ID** is 1130059476, our link is `https://itunes.apple.com/app/id11359476`. Use this information for the **Review Link** field in the **Project Settings** for iOS in Buildbox. It should look like this:

So, to summarize where we are and why we did things this way... we had to export and compile a test (just so we can export and compile again). This is so we can get our App ID from the iTunes Connect interface to populate our Review Link, and to set up our leaderboards. Again... thanks, Apple. Now, before we export our final, we just need to setup our store IDs.

Inside of the Coin Shop UI (in Buildbox), for each of our purchase buttons, set up the **Store Identifier** fields as follows:

- **10,000 Credit Purchase button**: com.audronis.rover10k
- **100,000 Credit Purchase button**: com.audronis.rover100k
- **Remove All Ads Purchase button**: com.audronis.roverNoAd

Now we have references that we can use in all our stores for these items to complete the purchases, and we'll be able to set them up across all devices. *FINALLY!* We can now export this thing for iOS (for real this time).

The actual build and upload to iTunes

Before we do this, go ahead and close xCode on your Mac, and delete all the previous export folders (on the Mac – and PC if you're using one). We don't want to accidentally upload anything that is incomplete. Now, *MAKE SURE YOU SAVE YOUR BUILDBOX PROJECT*. Although I've never had Buildbox crash during an export, it would be a crying shame to lose everything *now*.

Follow the same process as before:

1. In Buildbox, go to **File** | **Export** | **iOS**.
2. Copy the export folder to your Mac (if working on a PC).
3. Double-click the **PTPlayer.xcodeproj** file to open it in xCode.
4. Click on the **PTPlayer** entry on the left-side of xCode.
5. Select your iTunes account from the **Team** field.

In previous versions of Buildbox and xCode, you had to tick the **Requires Full Screen** checkbox, and then under **Build Settings** make sure **Enable Bitcode** was turned off (we're going to assume you're using the current version of xCode). Now, these should be set by default.

Before we upload this thing, we need to set our *scheme* from a specific device to Generic iOS Device. This is done at the very top of the xCode window. Just click on whatever device name is currently in there (that is, **iPhone 6s**) and a drop-down menu will appear where you can choose Generic iOS Device. There is no indication that a drop-down menu is there. So, if you don't know about this… you're left scratching your head wondering "Why can't I do this?" Thanks Apple. We drew a red box around the area we are talking about and how it should look in the following screenshot:

Now go to the top of the screen, and select **Product | Archive**. This will compile the build and prepare it for upload. After it completes, you'll get the following interface:

If you have multiple games on the iTunes store, you'll see a list of games on the left. Make sure the proper one is selected (**Ramblin Rover**), and click **Upload to App Store**. Just follow any requestors and use default settings at this point. If you get any provisioning errors, either click **Reset** (if available), or refer back to that section of this chapter to see where you may have gone wrong. This is the point I like to call *the pucker moment*. This is where anything that *can* go wrong will. Once you get the following screen, you can let out a sigh of relief, and go on to the iTunes Connect web page for this app. Occasionally, you will get the *failed to upload* ambiguous error. This is due to the traffic at iTunes Connect. Really, this means it could not validate the upload, so before trying again, go to iTunes Connect, and see if your build is there. If you *do* have to do it again… you'll need to increment your version number and build number first (back on the General tab of xCode), and re-archive:

Final setup in iTunes Connect

On the **App Information** screen, make sure you set the primary Category to Games, and the secondary to Arcade. Whenever you change a field, make sure to click the **Save** button at the top-right of the interface.

In-App Purchases I

Now, go to **Features**, and we'll add our **In-App Purchases** (using the little + icon next to **In-App Purchases**). Select **Consumable** as the type. Assign the following values to the following fields:

- **Reference Name**: `10,000 Credits` (this is a reference displayed to the developer for reporting)
- **Product ID**: `com.audronis.rover10k` (the same identifier from the Store Identifier field in the Buildbox interface for the purchase button)
- **Cleared for Sale**: `Yes` (if you tick **No**, people will no longer be able to purchase this item)
- **Price Tier**: `Tier 1` (this is the $0.99 price tier. You'll see a grid pop up to indicate how much items cost as you select each tier in just about every currency imaginable)
- **Add Language:**
    - **Language**: `English`
    - **Display Name**: `10,000 in-game Credits` (this is what users will see when they go to check out)
    - **Description**: `This will instantly add 10,000 credits to your balance.` (this is the description players will see when they check out)

For the **Screenshot for Review**, we are going to use the file in the content directory `SubmissionPix/iOS/StoreScreenshot.png`. The resolution requirements are strict on any images to Apple. If you get it wrong, don't worry... the image requirements come up with the error message. It *would* be nice if they told you *before* you got it wrong (rather than just giving a minimum resolution in the description). Again... thanks Apple. Click **Save**, and you're done.

Now just do the same with the 100,000 credits (using the `com.audronis.rover100k` **Product ID**, and substituting 100,000 where appropriate). Also, the **Price Tier** for this one is `Tier 5` ($4.99).

Finally, we add the **Remove all Ads** button. *THIS IS* A NON-CONSUMABLE (as it can be restored later, and only needs to be bought once). The values are as follows:

- **Reference Name**: `Remove all Ads`
- **Product ID**: `com.audronis.roverNoAd`
- **Cleared for Sale**: `Yes`

- **Price Tier**: `Tier 1`
- **Language**:
  - **Language**: `English`
  - **Display Name**: `Remove all Ads`
  - **Description**: `This will instantly remove all advertisements in the game.`

Of course, use the same store screenshot for all three of these. It should look like this when finished:

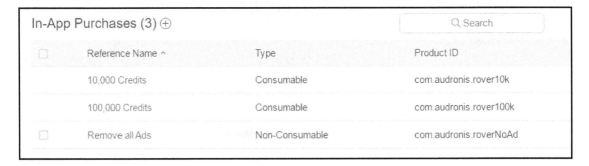

Now, on the top, go back to **App Store**, and select **Pricing and Availability** (left side). Set the **Price** to `USD 0 (Free)`. Now, buckle up, because the **1.0 Prepare for Submission** section is certainly a highway…

1.0 prepare for submission

iOS submission is strict to say the least. Let's take a look at each section one by one…

Version Information

The first thing you'll notice in this section is an area to upload screenshots for every single device offered by Apple iOS. **You must upload at least one screenshot at the appropriate resolution for every type of device.** Even though the game *should* look the exact same on every device, we have to do this before we can submit the game. Again… thanks Apple. Are you beginning to see why there are *a lot* of indie developers that give up on Apple iOS (or at least *hate* developing for Apple)? Again though…one of the biggest distribution channels around, so what are you going to do?

As our game is in a landscape (widescreen) aspect, we're listing the larger number as first in resolutions. However, if you make a portrait (tall) game, just switch the two numbers, and that will be your target resolution for screenshots. As we'll be taking screenshots from our Preview function within Buildbox, we're giving resolutions without the iOS status bar. If you'd like more resolution listings (with status bar), just click the **iOS Screenshot Properties** link on the Prepare for Submission page.

The following table shows the acceptable resolutions for devices (at the time of writing... there will be more with future iOS devices):

iOS Device Screen Size	Resolution of image (must be PNG of JPG)
3.5-inch retina display	960 x 600
4-inch retina display	1136 x 600
4.7-inch retina display	1334 x 750
5.5-inch retina display	2208 x 1242
iPad	2048 x 1536
iPad Pro	2732 x 2048

OK... so we get it. A LOT of screenshots to do. Lucky for you, we've created all the screenshots for Ramblin' Rover (you can create them by just clicking the camera icon in the Preview window of Buildbox, then adjusting the resolutions in your favorite photo-manipulation software).

Upload the pictures contained in the content directory
`SubmissionPix/iOS/Screenshots` (and the appropriate folders) to the appropriate
device previews, and put them (just drag them in iTunes Connect) in the order shown here:

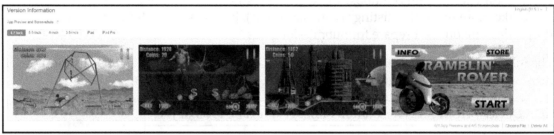

Now we fill out the rest of this section's form as follows:

- **Description**: Explore three planets with your rovers. Drive, jump, flip, and shoot
  your way as far as you can possibly go. Be careful though... some aliens are
  friendlier than others, some rovers are easier to drive than others, and the planets
  are completely different!

- **Controls**: Use buttons on the interface to drive, shoot, and jump. To flip in the air,
  rotate the device to lean and do front and backflips. Some rovers' jump jets hold
  more jumps than others. If you run out, you can recharge your jump jets by
  performing a flip in the air.

- **Keywords**: (This is what users will be able to search by, so we include some
  misspellings): `ramblin, ramblin', rambling, rambelin, rover, rovar,
  driving, motocross, shooter, shooting, alien.`

- **Support URL:** `http://www.audronis.com` (this is the URL to your website or
  Facebook

- **Marketing URL:** page for the game).
  Marketing URL: (link to the page where there is information about your game...
  this is optional, so we'll leave this blank).

On to the next section...

Build

Here, all you have to do is select the version you uploaded. Every version that has been uploaded and passed (sometimes the passing can take a day or two, but most often it's within minutes) can be selected here. You should receive an e-mail (in the email address associated with your iTunes account) indicating that the build has passed. Once selected, it should look as follows:

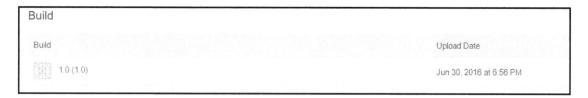

General app information

First, just upload an icon file (content directory `Projects/RamblinRover/misc/Icon-1024.png`). The resolution should be 1024 x 1024. For the **Copyright**, we enter a year, and the name of the copyright holder and it should be your full legal name (for Ramblin' Rover, it's `2016, Tyris M. Audronis`).

AS for the **Trade Representative Contact Information**, this is in case you are a corporation; it gives contact information for people to contact you through the Korean App Store. We'll leave this one blank.

The **Routing App Coverage File** is completely optional, and is a text file in GeoJSON format that restricts where your app is available (for instance, if it allows gambling, and you would like to make it unavailable where gambling laws apply). We'll leave this alone (as we want this game available *everywhere*).

Finally, the **Rating**. This is where Apple determines what game rating to assign to the game by filling out a questionnaire. You MUST be accurate (or the review team will reject the app). These are the form fields for Ramblin' Rover:

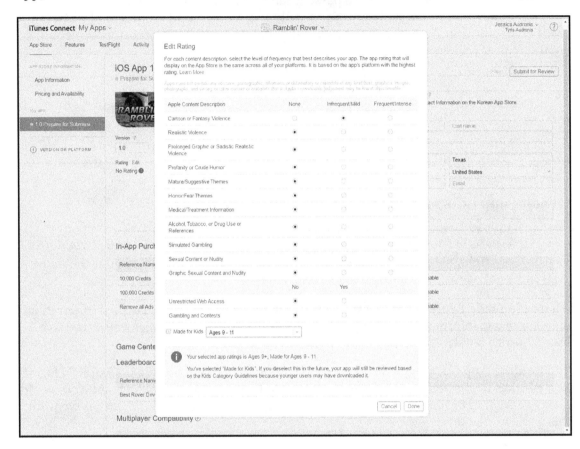

Notice we left **Made for Kids** unchecked. This is because (at the time of writing), Buildbox has no provision for a **Parental Gate**. A Parental Gate is a method by which a child cannot make a purchase without parental permission (and simply having to enter an iTunes password is not enough for Apple). So, because we have In-App Purchases... we cannot currently tick **Made for Kids**. Buildbox support does promise that they're hoping to include a parental gate in future versions, so hopefully by the time you read this... that has changed. After all... having that **Made for Kids** tag can really help with your download count.

We're going to need a privacy policy as well. There are several services that can host a privacy policy. Remember, we're serving up RevMob ads here, so make sure your privacy policy includes this. We used iubenda to generate and host ours (`http://www.iubenda.com`).

In-App Purchases II – and creating a revised version of the app

As we have In-App Purchases, it's imperative that we include a **Restore Purchases** button (or else due to current rules, it will be rejected). It's simple. In Buildbox, just add a **Navigation** button to the coin store using the `RestorePurchases.png` image (in the `Buttons` folder), and set its **Function** to `Restore Purchases`. Why didn't we say this before? Because it's also important to know how to generate a revision version of your app (as these kinds of issue pop up occasionally – especially with iTunes). It's virtually guaranteed that there will be a few *oops I forgot* moments, and you definitely need to know how to update versions. Keeping up with policies is a weekly task that you should make the time to keep up with (or else you may find your apps have been removed from the stores).

Generating a new version of your app

After adding the **Restore Purchases** button to your coin store, just go into the Project Settings window and set the **Version** to `1.01`. Now just export the new version, copy it to your Mac, and run another Archive procedure to upload the new version to the iTunes Connect account. Finally, in iTunes Connect, delete (by clicking on the – icon that pops up when you hover over the build) the 1.0 build, and then add the 1.01 build (the same way as before). Now, moving on...

Click the little + icon next to **In-App Purchases** and select all of the purchases that we set up earlier, as shown in the following screenshot, and then click **Done**:

Add In-App Purchases

Select In-App Purchases for us to review with this app version. The In-App Purchases shown below are the only ones in the Ready to Submit state. We only show free subscriptions in the Ready to Submit state here if your app version is in the Magazines & Newspapers category.

	Reference Name ˅	Product ID	Type
☑	10,000 Credits	com.audronis.rover10k	Consumable
☑	100,000 Credits	com.audronis.rover100k	Consumable
☑	Remove all Ads	com.audronis.roverNoAd	Non-Consumable

Cancel   Done

Game center

Turn on the switch next to the **Game Center** heading, and add the leaderboard that we set up earlier, in the same way we just added the In-App Purchases.

App review information

Just add your contact information here. This is in case the review team has any questions for you that must be answered before they clear it for sale. Under **Demo Account**, just untick the checkbox. This is only if we've set up something in the code where a demo account can be used without having to purchase anything. As we have no such feature, just untick this and move on.

Version release

Here is where you can select whether or not to manually or automatically release the game after Apple reviews your app. You can also schedule a release. Just leave this set on **Automatically release this version**.

Just click **Save**, then click **Submit for Review** (at the top of the page). Now it's just a matter of saying that no copyrights have been infringed upon, and letting Apple know that yes... we do use all IDFA possibilities for RevMob. Yes, RevMob does target ads, and also does track purchases used in the ads (and that's how you get paid). So make sure everything under IDFA is checked. Once you submit... WE'RE DONE!!!

It's all in the hands of Apple now. You just have to wait and see if it gets approved! WHEW! Let's move on now to other distribution channels (which are FAR simpler than iTunes)...

Great timing too (as it can take upwards of a week to get your approval).

Ok... one more just for fun... Thanks Apple.

Exporting and compiling for Google Play

First things first: let's download the compiler for Android. We're going to need to download and install the **Java Developer Kit (JDK)** version 7 (`http://www.oracle.com/technetwork/java/javase/downloads/jdk7-downloads-18826.html`).

Also, we're going to need the **Android Developer Tools (ADT)** bundle. Here are the links for various development platforms:

- **Mac:** `http://dl.google.com/android/adt/adt-bundle-mac-x86_64-21472.zip`
- **Windows (64-bit):** `http://dl.google.com/android/adt/adt-bundle-windows-x86_64-21472.zip`
- **Windows (32-bit):** `http://dl.google.com/android/adt/adt-bundle-windows-x86-21472.zip`

Once you get these installed, make sure you have an Internet connection, and start Eclipse. It will prompt you for selecting a *Workspace*. A workspace is simply an area on your hard drive where Eclipse can store a project, and all related settings. Then, from the top menu, select **Window | Android SDK Manager**. Now it's time to install the packages that Eclipse needs to compile for Android. Install **Android 6.0 (API 23)**. If you get error messages (telling you that something can't install because a different package must be installed first)... simply install the packages that Eclipse is asking for and then install API 23. There are occasional updates to these packages, so you'll need to open Android SDK Manager every so often to download updates. It should look like this when downloading:

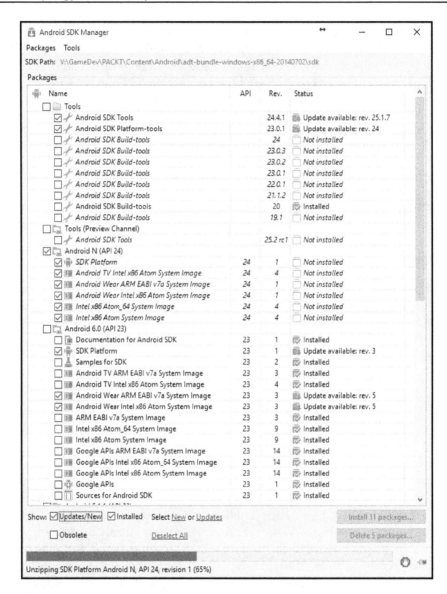

Ok… now it's time to export and compile! Don't forget to grab the **Leaderboard ID** from Google Play's game services and include it in the Project Settings within Buildbox for Google Play.

Don't forget to select **Google Play** from the **Application Store** drop-down menu before entering this information.

Then… just select **File** | **Export** | **Android**. After selecting a location on your hard drive to export your project, just wait a minute (again, no progress bar) for the export. Once it finishes… move over to Eclipse.

Compiling in Eclipse

After xCode and iTunes Connect, you may be scarred. Ok… maybe not, but the point is that Eclipse and Google Play are *FAR* easier to get going. So don't stress, here we go.

Inside Eclipse, select **File** | **Import**, and select **Existing Android Code into Workspace** (as shown in the following screenshot, on the left). Like we said before, when Buildbox exports, it actually outputs the code that a compiler uses to create an executable package (in most cases). On the next screen, navigate to where you exported your Buildbox project, and select the Android folder (as shown in the following screenshot, on the right). Eclipse will detect what the code is, and represent it on this screen. Click **Finish** to move on:

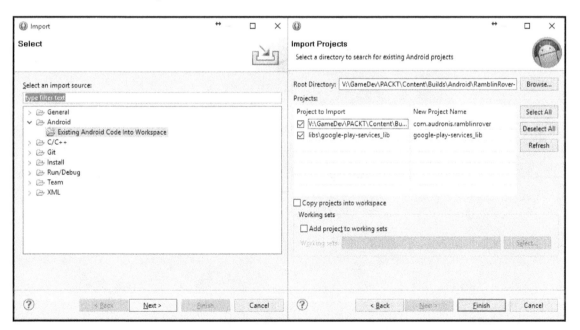

Lint is a tool that Eclipse uses to check for potential bugs in code. Lint is not compatible with Buildbox code, and will not let you compile if it's allowed to check for errors. To disable it, right-click on the main package (on the left side of Eclipse… in this case, `com.audronis.ramblinrover`) and select **Properties**. On the following interface, select **Android Lint Preferences**, and then click on **Ignore All**. Click **OK** to move on. It should look like the following screenshot:

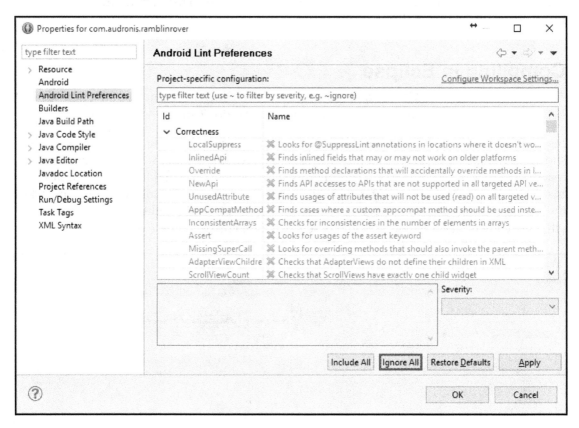

Now we get to compile it! Again, right-click on your main application, but this time select **Android Tools | Export Signed Application Package**. You can just click **Next** through the first screen of the interface (see the following screenshot, on the left). This just verifies that this is the application you want to compile. On the next screen, you'll need to create a signing key (to verify that it is in fact you that is creating new versions of your apps and to prevent others from reverse-engineering them). It's simple... just select a location on your hard drive to store your key, and then create a password (that you'll remember). Also, remember where you stored the key, because you can reuse it whenever you compile anything for Android. It should look something like the screenshot on the right:

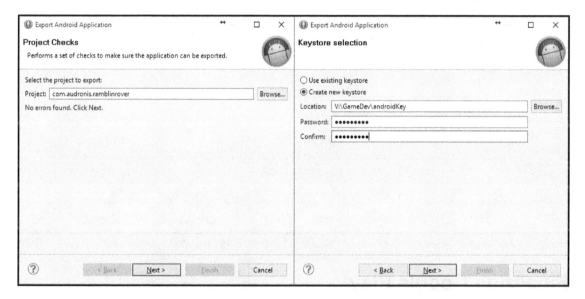

The next screen only appears when creating a new key. Just fill out the form, and put a ridiculously large number in the **Validity** field. This is how long your key is good for. We put in the maximum (1000 years). It should look like the left side of the following screenshot. And finally, just select where you want the compiled file (also known as an APK) and we're done with the compile! This screen is shown on the right side of the following screenshot:

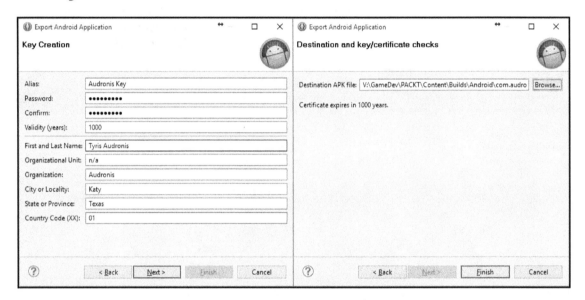

Finalizing Google Play

Now we just need to get everything setup in our store so people can download our game! Let's start by uploading our game…

Uploading the APK

Back in your Google Play Developer Console, go to the APK screen (**All Applications | Ramblin Rover | APK**). After uploading your APK file (by clicking **Upload New APK to Production**), the interface should look like this:

From here on, it's fairly self-explanatory. So, let's go through this quickly; on to the **Store Listing**.

The Store Listing

We filled out the **Store Listing** as follows:

- **Title:** Ramblin' Rover
- **Short Description:** Explore planets with different rovers to find a new home for humanity
- **Full Description:** (We used the same one from our iTunes listing)
- **Graphic Assets:** (Luckily, the format restrictions here are not nearly as strict as iTunes, so we just used all the same assets from our iOS 5.5 inch listing)
- **Hi-res icon:** (We used the 512×512 icon in the misc folder within our project)
- **Feature Graphic:** (1024×500 image from the same folder)
- **Promo Graphic:** (180×120 image from the same folder)
- **TV Banner:** (1280×720 image from the same folder)
- **Promo Video:** (Link to YouTube video of the gameplay. If you have an nVidia video card, you can easily record this with your preview window in Buildbox using nVidia Shadowplay)
- **Application Type:** Games

- **Category**: Arcade
- **Content Rating**: (Leave blank)
- **Website**: (Your website URL here)
- **Privacy Policy**: (Link to same privacy policy from iTunes)

Content rating

Follow the simple questionnaire on the content rating section. It should be noted that since you have a store and advertising, it is extremely important that you check *yes* to all questions regarding advertising, sharing location, sharing information, and In-App Purchases (or else you may find your app banned).

After completing the **Content Rating** section, go back to the **Store Listing** and apply your rating (you know you're done if after saving a green checkmark appears next to **Store Listing**).

Again, just fill out the questionnaire. Make sure you select free, distribute to all available countries, and specify that it contains ads. Also, when saved, a green checkmark will appear next to **Pricing & Distribution**.

In-App products

For each of your In-App Purchases, add a new **Managed Product** using the same Product IDs from Buildbox (that is, com.audronis.rover10k for the 10,000 credit purchase). Once you've created the product, you can now input all the necessary information as follows:

- **Title**: Enter the title of the purchase (10,000 in-game Credits, 100,000 in-game Credits, and so on).
- **Description**: We used the same descriptions from the iTunes store (*Instantly gives you...*).
- **Pricing Template**: This only applies if you have created a template based on previous pricing... if you haven't, leave this blank.

- **Price**: All you need to do is fill out one country's price, and the rest is filled in based on exchange rates provided by Google. We entered our price for the United States, and all other prices were filled in for us. Just make sure you tick the checkbox at the top of the form, as follows:

Here is where we're going to link up to Google Play services for our leaderboards. Just click on the button Use Play Game Services, and select Ramblin Rover game services. The SHA1 certificate code from when you compiled the game will automatically be set in the appropriate fields, so all you need to do is click through until you can get to the Game Details for your leaderboards again. We're just going to finish this up.

Game Details

Fill out this form using the same high-res icon from the main game, and the same feature graphic as well. On the **Description**, we said `Who's the best driver? Compare your distance scores with other players here`. It's important to just have a brief description of what the leaderboard is. After saving, you should have a green checkmark for **Game Details**. All we should need now is achievements, testing, and publishing.

Achievements

In order to publish an app with leaderboards, you must have at least five achievements based on score. We're going to use Naval ranks for this (as it's popular in Sci-Fi to have Naval ranks associated with space-faring ranks). We'll go from Ensign through Captain (6 ranks in total) using images we put in the misc folder in our content directory. We filled them out as follows:

Name	Description	Icon	Points	List Order
Ensign (Trainee)	Congratulations, you know how to drive a rover!	Ensign.png	5	1
Lieutenant (Junior-Grade)	Congrats! You are no longer a total noob!	LtJG.png	25	2
Lieutenant	You're almost a professional now!	LT.png	50	3
Lieutenant-Commander	You are now the go-to guy. So, go get 'em!	LtCMDR.png	100	4
Commander	Alright, sir. You're getting downright salty!	CMDR.png	150	5
Captain	Well, you've done it! You're now the man in charge. Everyone now calls you "the old man."	CAPTAIN.png	200	6

At this point... you're done! Just keep clicking **Continue to Next Step**, and then click on **Publish your game**. And that's it... no approval process. Just about half an hour of effort, and it's up and ready to download!

Exporting and compiling for Amazon App Store

Getting up on Amazon is almost the same as Google Play. There are just a few minor differences. In your **Amazon Developer** console, you should see text at the top that says **GameCircle**. Click on this to add the Amazon leaderboard for your game. The first step looks like the following:

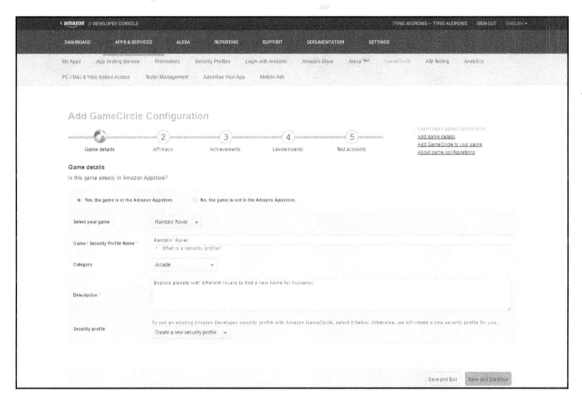

Now, before we export from Buildbox, add the Leaderboard ID of your choosing for Amazon in the **Buildbox Project Settings** for Amazon. Unlike the other distribution channels, you can use a Leaderboard ID of your choosing (we used `roverLeaderboard`). We'll have to compile it in Eclipse to get our MD5 key. Follow the same process as with Google Play to export and compile in Eclipse (with the exception of exporting as Amazon instead of Android). The final step on the Eclipse compile will show your MD5 and SHA1 keys (generated by Eclipse). On the next screen for GameCircle, you'll need to enter your MD5 key when you generate your new API key. The result looks like this:

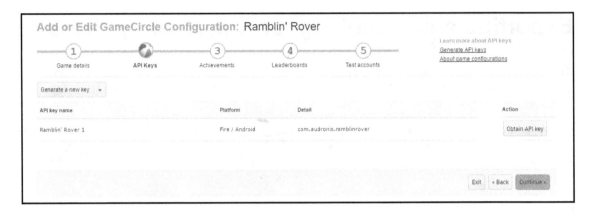

Now we move on to creating the actual leaderboard. Unlike all of the other distribution channels, you can name your Leaderboard ID yourself. When you go to add a leaderboard, the form should be filled out as follows:

The rest of the submission forms are very similar to Google Play. Just fill them out, and don't forget to add your In-App Purchases.

> For Amazon In-App Purchases, use your Store Identifier from Buildbox for each item in the SKU field.

Exporting and compiling for the Windows store

Before we get started exporting, there are some alterations we're going to need to make. First off, you may remember that the only ads available are provided via Vungle (and not our currently installed RevMob). So, you're going to want to save a new copy of your project, and go back to replace all of the ads on your UIs with Vungle ads.

Another key difference is that with In-App Purchases, you must set the **Content Type** for your purchase to `Electronic Software Download` within the Microsoft Developer Center console. And of course, the removal of ads would be a **Durable**, and the coins would be a **Consumable**. Since you already know the principles of submitting an app by now, we'll leave the particulars of the store alone (all app submissions require similar processes). Instead, let's focus on the compiling of the package for the store. Know that you must create your store entry BEFORE you compile, though.

Compiling with Visual Studio

If you don't already have Microsoft Visual Studio, you can download it here: `https://www.visualstudio.com/en-us/downloads/download-visual-studio-vs.aspx`. There is a free version (Visual Studio Community), and it will work just fine for our purposes. Once it's installed, here is the process:

1. From Buildbox, export for Windows Store to a temporary folder on your desktop. For some reason, if you export to another drive, you may run into permission errors.
2. Inside of the export directory, double-click on the file `BBPlayer.sfn` to open the Visual Studio project that Buildbox created.
3. Within Visual Studio, on the top menu, select **Project | Store | Edit App Manifest**:

   1. Click on the **Packaging** tab.

2. Click on the **Choose Certificate** button.

3. From the **Configure Certificate** dropdown, select `Create Test Certificate`.

4. Enter your company name (or your name) and then click through the **OK**s and **YES**s until you are back on the main Visual Studio Screen.

4. From the top menu, select **Project | Store | Associate App with Store**:

   1. Log in with your Microsoft Store credentials.

   2. Select the app entry you created in the Microsoft Store.

   3. Clean the project (and go back to the main interface by selecting **OK**).

5. From the top menu, select **Project | Store | Create App Packages**, and follow the defaults clicking `Next`. It will take a little while to compile.

6. When it's finished compiling, click on the **Launch Windows App Certification Kit** and let it run through your app (it will take some time to complete).

Now you'll have a folder called **AppPackages** inside of the exported project folders. The file with the `.appxupload` extension is your final compiled package for upload to the Windows Store. After everything is complete and you've submitted your app, this is what your Windows Store interface should look like:

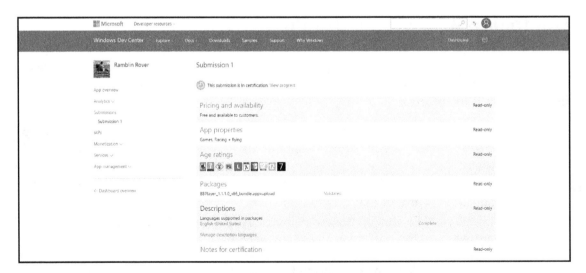

Exporting and compiling for Steam

The first thing you should do is get on Steam Greenlight. As we've said before, you must get approved before you can even upload your app. So, at Steam Greenlight, you'll need to upload photos of your game and describe what it is. Some people even use animated gifs to show gameplay. Be creative; tell a story in your descriptions. Unfortunately, you don't have the chance for users to download a demo of the game, so these images and descriptions need to make people really want to play your game.

Just remember this: Apple is a great example. Their hardware is no different than a Windows machine. The Apple OS is Linux-based, so nearly no difference there. But why does everyone want an Apple? Why can they charge more for it? Marketing.

Know your audience, and try to captivate their interest and get the users to vote for your game. Finally, there are A LOT of games on Greenlight… *stand out*.

Adjusting your game for Steam

Steam is a bit different than other distribution channels. First… no ads. Steam does not allow games to have ads at this time. So that could cut into your profits in a serious way. Also, Steam does support In-App Purchases, but there are two potential issues:

- Documentation on the actual implementation of In-App Purchases is limited. So, count on having some possible issues with this.
- In-App Purchases are *only* allowed on free-to-play games. So, our potential profits are going down fast.

With all that in mind, here's my suggestion: remove all ads, add more 100 credit pickups (or even an occasional 1,000), charge $0.99 for the app, and finally lower the price of the Phoenix rover to 50,000 credits.

These adjustments will still generate some profits, make the Phoenix more attainable without spending money, and the price is still low enough so that players may even buy it just to check it out.

Compiling for Steam using Visual Studio

The export for Steam is pretty straightforward in Buildbox. The same process of **File** | **Export**, and then select Steam. Since we're again using Visual Studio, make sure you compile to a temporary folder on the desktop (or else you may end up with permission errors when you go to compile).

Now, on the desktop go to the folder you exported from Buildbox and double-click the `PTPlayer.sfn` file. Compiling is actually very simple for Steam using Visual Studio. You just have to make sure to use the right Platform Toolset.

While in Visual Studio, right-click on the **PTplayer** entry in the Solution Editor window (top-right) and select `Properties`. We just need to make sure that Visual Studio understands what version of Visual Studio that our exported project is for. Now, under **Platform Toolset**, select `Visual Studio 2013 (v120)` from the drop-down menu, as shown in the following screenshot:

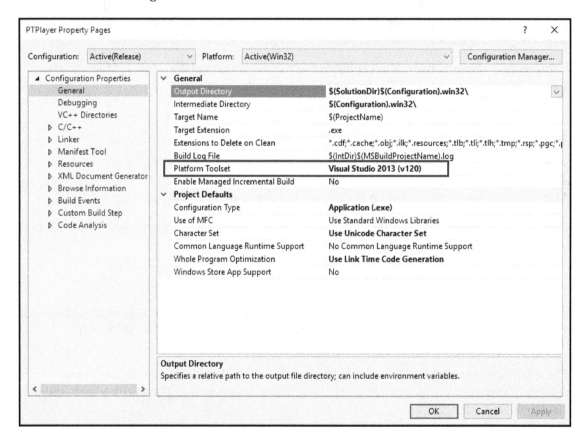

If you don't have this option, you'll have to close Visual Studio, and run the installer for Visual Studio again. When given the chance, click the **Modify** button during install, and add the necessary component. If you're not sure which components to install, the easiest course of action is to just install them all (make sure everything is checked). Then, after installing the components, return and set the **Platform Toolset** to `Visual Studio 2013 (v120)`.

Only one more step to take: on the top menu, select **Build** | **Build PTPlayer**. A lot of text will scroll by in the bottom window. This is Visual Studio compiling your final result. You'll know it's finished (and has succeeded) if the bottom line of the text reads as follows:

```
========== Build: 1 succeeded, 0 failed, 0 up-to-date, 0 skipped ==========
```

Final Steam notes

Steam Greenlight could use some improvements for sure. It's a relatively new distribution channel. As a result, the process is a bit odd (with offering no downloadable previews of the game, and only a few Steam users even know it exists to go vote for games). Unless you have a lot of friends, loved ones, or associates that can go vote for you... you might find your app completely ignored.

Don't be discouraged if this happens. You'll find that sometimes the projects that are greenlit are projects that are not necessarily the best games.

So, you may be wondering why we even bother covering Steam at all. Steam (regular) is a very popular place for players to buy games; and with the outcry from indie developers for Steam to fix their process, you may see the need to compile for Steam sooner rather than later (as they probably will make adjustments to help).

So, although it's not (currently) an optimal distribution channel, you should be versed and ready on the compilation process for Steam. After all, the day may come soon where Steam is the *go to* for indie developers.

Summary

Well, there we have it! A complete game, adjusted and compiled for distribution channels, and live so that people can download and play it. A lot of work, and a lot of nuances and complexity in this chapter. Hopefully, you now know how various distribution channels work and their commonalities so that you can easily navigate through any new channels that may pop up as well.

In this chapter, we learned all about distribution channels. We dealt with all of the complexity of compiling, preparing, and submitting for the Apple iOS store (iTunes). We also breezed through Google Play, and the slightly more difficult Amazon App Store. We then moved into PC gaming with the Windows store, and even covered Steam. If this chapter took you the longest to get through, don't worry. The entire process of submitting Ramblin' Rover to all of these channels took over three weeks to complete (when the game itself took less time to create).

But consider this… Buildbox has done such a great job of making game creation easy, that the hardest part of getting your game out to players is actually distributing it! As we covered in our introduction to Buildbox, this is what makes it revolutionary. This is what makes Buildbox a great tool for creating simple games very quickly. Now, if only distribution channels would streamline their processes a bit more, right?

Starting in the next chapter, we're going to wind down our pace a bit. We'll be covering how the process of building a game will be a bit different for some of the other types of game presets within Buildbox. We'll also cover making entirely new types of game (such as the popular mobile game **Color Switch** - made with Buildbox). We'll even get into some of the principles of making Isometric (2.5d) games.

Ready? Let's go!

8
Building Other Popular Game Types

As we've said many times previously, there are a ton of different types of games you can make with Buildbox. We could quite literally make an encyclopaedia about the intricacies of each one. But that's not our purpose here. Our goal is to get you familiar with how Buildbox works and all of the driving principles behind it, and then show you some of the potential. This will hopefully get you thinking and inventing new ways to use Buildbox on your own (rather than just copying what we do, and what others have done). So, here's to you taking Buildbox to the next level! Shall we get started with some other examples?

Isometric (2.5D) games with Buildbox

Isometric (ISO) games are ones that are still presented two-dimensionally, but do represent a third dimension (depth). This would be games such as *Qubert* (`https://itunes.apple.com/us/app/qbert-rebooted/id1010883120?mt=8`), *ZAXXON* (`http://www.classic-retro-games.com/games/shooters/zaxxon-70`), the original *Legend of Zelda*, and so on. ISO games are also called 2.5D (two-and-a-half D) because although they resemble a 3D game, they still work and behave like a 2D game. ISO games add a bit of realism, and a whole other dimension of complexity to game play.

The initial setup for an ISO game is simple. When you're setting up your game, just choose either **ISO Jump** or **ISO Jump Slide** from the **Gameplay Settings** area of the **Creator** screen, as shown in the following screenshot:

The first thing you're going to notice with an ISO game in Buildbox is that right off the bat, everything looks a bit cockeyed. Even the stage is tilted to the left. This has to do with the direction that the game will scroll (instead of from right to left, from upper-right to lower-left). So, because the game scrolls in this direction, the backgrounds and scenes extend in the direction of the scroll. You can see this in the following screenshot:

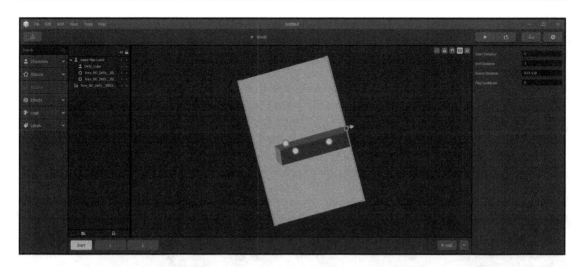

Now, let's take a quick look at how collision shapes work in ISOs. In the following screenshot, you'll notice that the graphic itself is level, and the object (an oblong cube) is slightly rolled forward rather than made with the same slant the stage has. This is a good practice because you'll most likely have to adjust its angle to match the stage anyway.

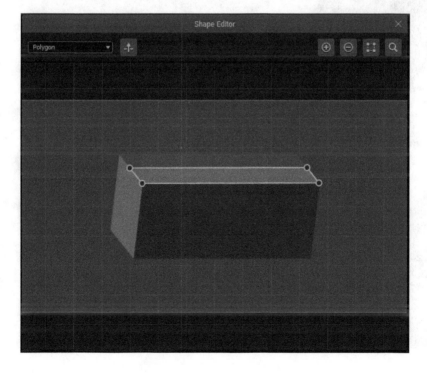

You'll also notice that the collision shape only takes up half of the top surface of this object. This is so that your character can move along the object directly on its center. It helps with the illusion of depth, and gives the perception that the character is actually on the surface.

Similarly, the character itself has a collision shape that takes the perspective of 2.5D into account. If there is an object above, it would hide the top surface of our character, and behind would hide the back surface of our character (making it important to keep the order of objects in relation to characters important in the Layers window). And, our character will overlap the collision area of objects below our character. Thus, we also align the bottom part of our collision shape with the center line of what our inferred bottom surface is. It looks like the following screenshot:

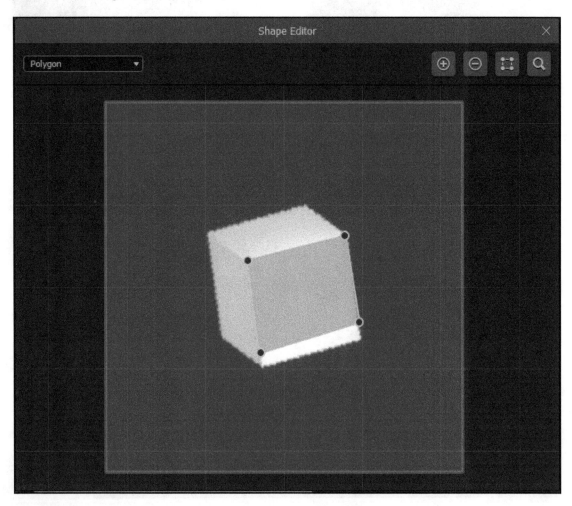

So, as you can see, the complexity level does go up a bit with ISO games. Furthermore, there are some other limitations. For instance, as the objects are still actually two-dimensional, if you try to make your character (or other objects) tumble, the results will just look…odd. So, you'll definitely want to get a different type of game under your belt before attempting an ISO game.

Abstract games (such as Color Switch)

First, let's say that in no way are the makers of *Color Switch* affiliated with this book. Nor is this section necessarily a statement on exactly how the game was made. Instead, we feel that *Color Switch* is an excellent example of an abstract game that was created with Buildbox. And yes, there are no doubt several ways in which you could make a game like this. However, this chapter (again) is designed to show you possibilities and get you thinking. Alrighty…now that the lawyers are happy, let's get into it.

First, let's start by making a Fall Buttons type game, and delete everything except the character (from the Asset Library). Also, delete any backgrounds from all the scenes. It should look like the following screenshot:

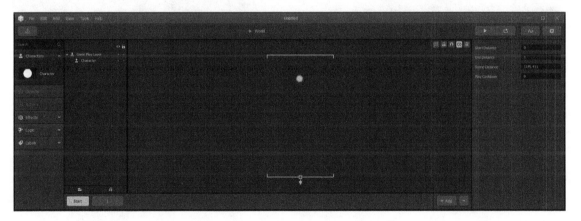

You'll want to adjust the settings of the character so that it can jump, and the settings of the world so that it moves from top to bottom. Where the secret lies with our version (called *Color Exchange* – clever, eh?) is with how the collision objects and actual switching of the character's color works…

What we use to create the collision for the color wheel is invisible colliders. The following screenshot shows how we have a spinning `no collide` object with a bunch of small rectangles lining the edge. These rectangles are children of the color wheel, and their **Destroy Type** is set to `Destroy Character`. Then, we just set the **Angular Velocity** of the color wheel to whatever makes sense to you (we used `60`). Also, notice that we left the green part of our color wheel without collider objects. This means it's our pass-through, so we're starting with a green ball on this scene.

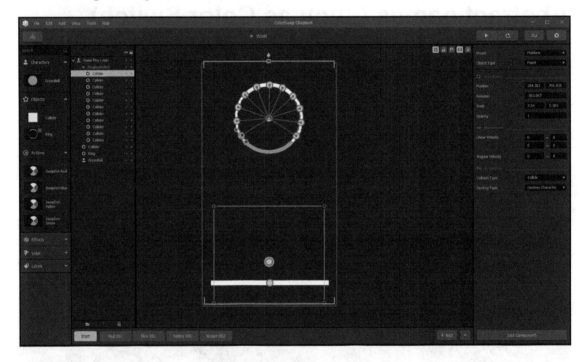

On our start screen here, you may also notice that we start with a non-destroying collider under the ball so that our players have a small amount of time before they need to start jumping the ball up the screen.

Then, on our other scenes, it's just a matter of changing the blank area of our rotating wheel to whatever color our ball is. To change the color of the ball, we use an action, and set an action animation to a new graphic that is the desired color of our ball with a `Replace` **Animation Behavior** and a **Duration** (of our animation) of `9999` (pretty much until we change it again). You can see all of this in the following screenshot:

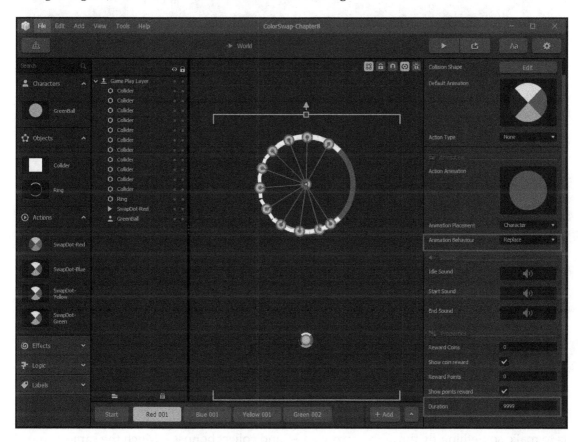

You can also see that we've created actions for red, blue, yellow, and green color exchanges. Now, it's just a matter of creating more scenes with color exchanges, and different gap-colors (that correspond to the color exchange). You can change the color-wheel's spin direction, size, and speed as you like to add some complexity and variance. Then, all we have to do is select our universal Collider object (from the Asset Library), and edit the Default Animation to make the **Opacity** 0. Blammo! Now the players can't see the colliders, and we have our Color Exchange game. All we have to do now is finalize our controls.

On the **World UI**, we just need to delete our left and right buttons, and create a new **Character Button** (with no graphic) that has a Jump Action and it takes up the whole screen. This makes it so that simply tapping the screen (anywhere on the screen) makes the character jump. It should look like the following screenshot:

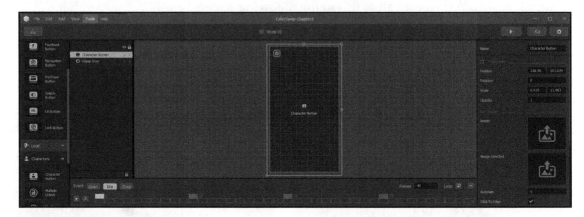

So, those are the secrets to creating an abstract game like *Color Switch*. Simple, right? Also, very quick to make. Some of the best games are extremely simple. The best-selling games all have one thing in common: originality. It's just a matter of figuring out a new way of manipulating your development platform (in this case, Buildbox) to make something new and inventive.

Flappy Bird – style games

Believe it or not, *Flappy Bird* was not actually the first game to use this sort of locomotion. *Joust* (from the old *Atari* game systems) was an instant hit with very similar flight methods.

It's very similar to making a platformer-style game (scrolls from right to left), but the object is to make something fly through narrow gaps, and collect bonuses. Much the same as our Color Exchange game, you keep a character in the air by repeatedly pushing the jump button.

The template in Buildbox for such games is pretty much just a matter of replacing objects and adding scenes. It's pre-made pretty well, extremely easy to complete, and makes for a great beginner project for your first solo-run.

Here is a screenshot from *Drone Challenge* (my first Buildbox game). I created and published it in less than two weeks (in time for a drone convention), and is the entire reason I started using Buildbox for quick-turnaround projects:

Running shooter and platformer games

Running shooters and platformers are very similar, so we've combined them here. The object of both is to make it as far as you can, while conquering obstacles and enemies. The difference is that with a running shooter, you can destroy your enemies by shooting at them. As you saw with Ramblin' Rover, we used elements of these types of games with our rovers (especially on our second and third worlds).

These games are extremely easy to make if you use Buildbox's pre-built templates. With Buildbox 2, and its new ability to have multiple worlds, the possibilities with these games are greatly expanded. They also make great first-timer projects.

Here is an image from *Chihua Hop*. It's another project I made (as a test of physics and changing characters with Buildbox 1.x). The Chihuahua has to make it through the houses and yards of the neighborhood while avoiding aliens and cats, and collecting treats. The Chihuahua fires…well, what everyone that owns a dog dreads.

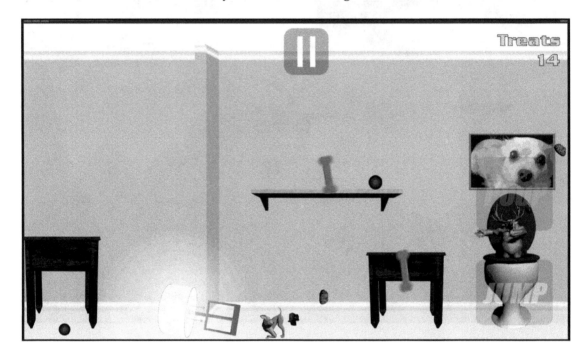

Space shooters

Space shooters can either scroll horizontally (such as *Gallaga*) or vertically (such as *Space Invaders*). These are another variety of game that can be both very easy to make and can be big sellers (due to their popularity).

For a *Gallaga,* style game, you'll want to use the `Side Shooter` template. The speed does scroll by super slow with the template, and you have to go all the way to the right side of the screen to advance the game faster (possibly resulting in crashing into obstacles). So, you'll want to bring your right barrier in about a third of the playing field before replacing your graphics to make the game more fun (as shown in the following screenshot). Also, consider speeding up the base-movement of the game by adjusting the **Forced Movement** parameters of the world(s).

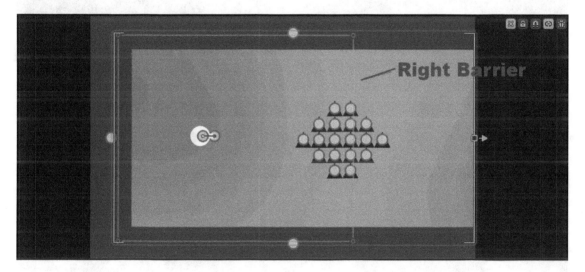

For a *Space Invaders* style game, the preset template we use will be `Dogfight`. It's a super slow game by default. So to make things more interesting, you may want the game to gradually increase speed (by again adjusting the **Forced Movement** parameters for our world). The **Force Increase** parameter increases your movement speed over time (from minimum to maximum). It's a touchy setting, so we've found that `0.05` is just about perfect for this type of game. Then, it's just a matter of setting the **Force Max** setting ridiculously high (so that no human could possibly keep up, or else the game will get boring). We set it to `400`. This is how we set it up:

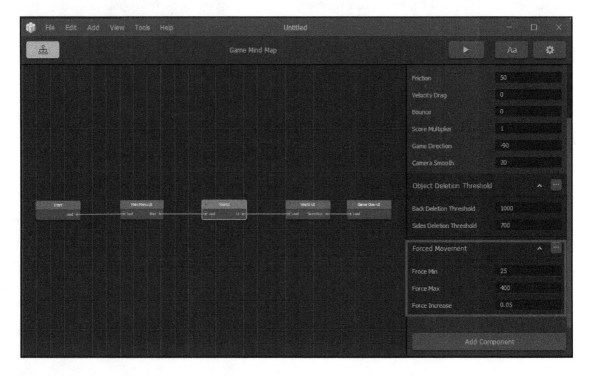

Finally, on the Bullet object, you'll probably want to set the **Velocity** much higher than the stock preset to keep up with the movement increase (as well as increase the **Spawn Rate**).

360 shooter games

The video game that started an explosion of arcades all across the world… *Asteroids* is probably the most famous 360 shooter game of all time. Can you top it? Actually, you just might be able to with Buildbox. *How is that possible,* you may ask. Because Buildbox's preset for 360 shooter games has combined the ability to spin your character and move with the scrolling screen and ever-changing environments of a side-shooter.

There really aren't a lot of tips to give here (as we covered that with the side-shooter game). However, there is a ton of potential for inventive moshing here. Imagine a 360 shooter where you're flying through blood vessels as a nanite (microscopic robot) shooting viruses! You may even be able to get a grant for such a game if you make it scientifically accurate and educational. I think I may have just come up with the idea for my next game. Bacteria Blast? Virus Vindicator? Hmm…

Being inventive doesn't just apply to the game mechanics. It is directly relevant to funding your game development (remember, Buildbox costs $100 a month with a year contract; then there's all the other costs for graphics software, music, and so on). It's also directly relevant to marketing. Imagine teachers in grade schools endorsing your game, or science museums implementing it on their museum floor.

Having a good business mind for marketing your game (while designing it) can be crucial to the success of your game in a saturated market.

Maze chompers (such as Pac Man)

What would any 2D game development guide be if we didn't tell you how to make (without a doubt) the most popular video game of all time? Songs were made about *Pac Man*, movies (such as the inclusion of Pac Man in Pixels), the first game with spin-offs, lines in video arcades. The whole world suffered from Pac Man fever for nearly five years!

So, how do you make a maze chomper in Buildbox? Well, believe it or not…there's a template for that as well. The template is called `Stage Clear`. Since we're getting a bit tired of the stock monochrome primitive graphics, we went ahead and replaced some of the graphics in our test project with elements that come with Buildbox.

The basic template does have a maze, coins, and a character to eat them. However, there are some key elements that are missing to make this a classic maze chomper game. We need to include some roaming enemies and teleport channels to make this more like the classic maze chomper games.

Before we do all that, we deleted all of our graphic assets from the Asset Library and built a maze that looks like this:

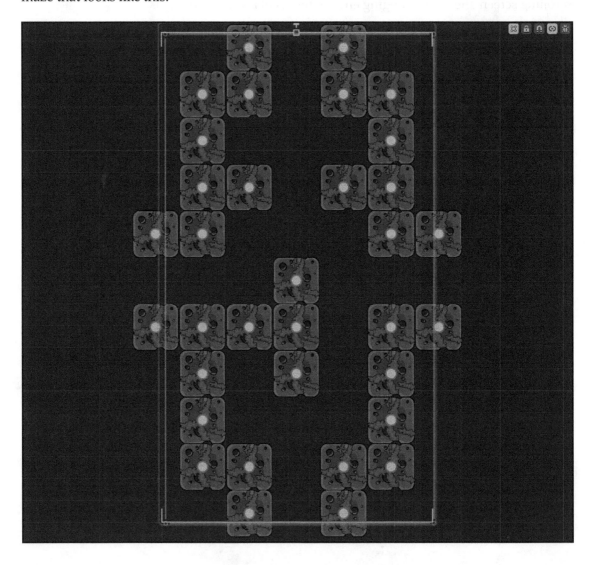

So, our gaming field is set for a scene, so now let's add a character and an enemy and start working on how to make that enemy roam around on the stage.

Roaming enemies

Unfortunately, there is no logic behavior (at this time) to make enemies chase characters (nor run from them). However, we can simulate this type of behavior by using the Transform object. Here's how we set it up.

In the following screenshot, you can see several transform objects placed around the map. You can also get an idea of how they change the movement of our enemy to send it roving around the map:

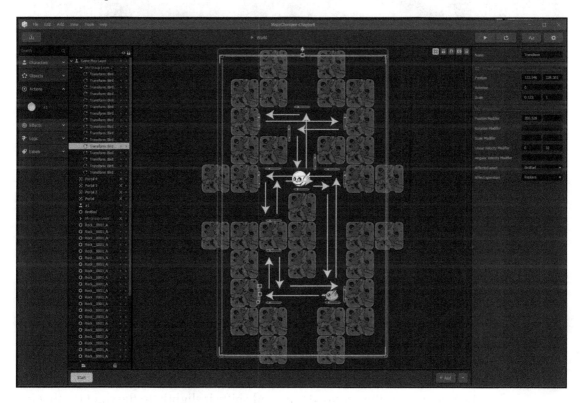

If the exact path doesn't make sense to you…that's ok. You don't need to see the specifics of every intersection of motion. What you do need to know is how we can have the same object (our enemy) traverse the same section of the map in different ways. So, let's take a look:

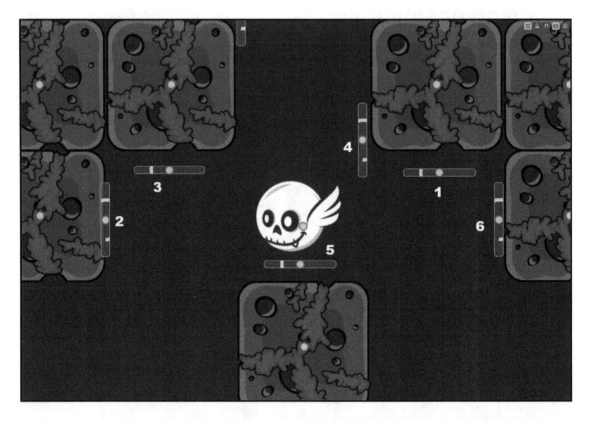

The preceding screenshot is one section of the stage. Ignore our character here…let's take a look at how we make our enemy move through this section:

1. Our enemy approaches this section from underneath and touches this bumper (which transforms the motion of the enemy to move left). Also, this bumper shifts the enemy down slightly so that it avoids bumper 3 and 4, while remaining above 5 as well.
2. This bumper moves the enemy down, and shifts it slightly to the right (so that it avoids re-touching this bumper on its way back up).
3. The enemy was sent down by bumper 2, and back up by an off-screen bumper. Once it hits bumper 3, the enemy moves to the right. Notice that bumper 3 is slightly higher than bumper 1.

4. Since our enemy is slightly higher than it was when it was sent left by bumper 1, it will now hit bumper 4 and be sent up to another section.

5. The enemy now returns to this section from the upper section (missing bumper 4 on its way back down, and is sent to the right by bumper 5).

6. Bumper 5 is low enough to send our enemy to the right and have it miss bumpers 4 and 1. When the enemy hits bumper 6, it's sent back to the lower section of the map to start its loop all over again.

And there it is... the easy way to have a roaming enemy. You can always add more enemies and either have them use the same bumpers, or ones that only work for them to add some complexity.

Now we just add some portals (two groups of two portals each), and drop some coins on the stage (that each have a reward of one coin) as shown here:

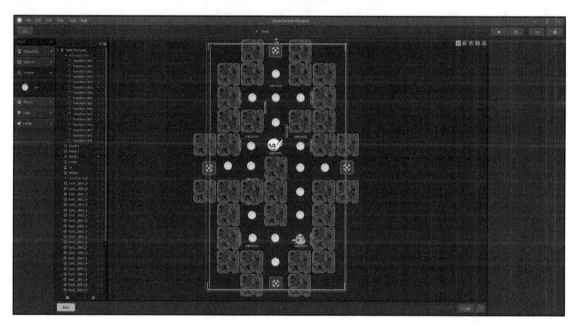

And, to finish it up, we need to know when all of the coins have been consumed by our character. On the UI screen, we just select our **All Coins** event listener and set the **Session Total** parameter to 19 (the number of coins on our screen). What we've done here is sensed how many coins our character has eaten, and triggered Game Over once they've eaten them all. This parameter is illustrated here:

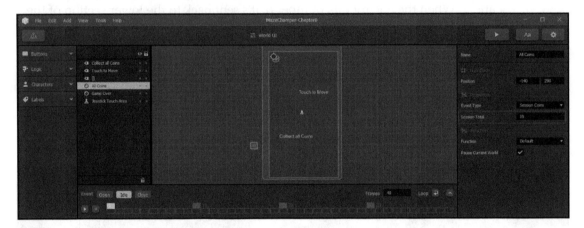

Summary

As you can see, there is a lot of potential inside Buildbox to create interesting games, inventive games, and even games that are a throw-back to the past. No matter what type of game you create, there is one thing that all game developers have in common: the ability to think about the inner workings of your project to create solutions within the confines of the development environment.

Well, that's pretty much it for explaining the development environment for Buildbox. In the next and final chapter, we're going to cover some more of the tips and tricks to Buildbox, provide checklists, and give you some quick references to help troubleshoot issues with your projects.

9
Buildbox Tips and Tricks

You've made it! In all of our previous chapters, you've learned about how to use Buildbox to make the games that are in your mind come to life on various devices. But it's a lot to remember, right? Well, we've got you covered. This chapter is going to be a quick reference to troubleshoot issues, and provides checklists to complete various tasks to make games with Buildbox.

Graphics optimization checklist

When creating the graphics, here are the important things to remember:

- Graphics may not be bigger than the Atlas size (2048×2048 by default)
- All graphics must be PNG format (8, 24, or 32-bit)
- PNGs with transparency should be 32-bit (24 with transparency), or you may end up with white outlines around your graphic
- Animations may be loaded as PNG image-sequences (up to 30 frames/sec)

Tips for reducing graphics load

So, let's say you get your game all finished, but it's over 100 MB (the limit for iOS and Android). You can do some things to reduce the asset load for your game, and one of these aspects is with the graphics. Here's the order that I look at things to begin trimming some fat off my projects:

1. **Have I optimized my assets within Buildbox?** Don't forget to follow the optimization procedures (removing unused assets via the **Tools** menu and optimizing and rebuilding your Atlas).

2. **Have I scaled my objects down?** Objects such as platforms, boulders, and enemies. If they've been scaled down within Buildbox, it may be a good idea to reduce the original graphic size and then replace my object's graphic with the reduced object.

3. **Do I need every frame of my image sequences?** Starting with enemies and other objects (and only adjusting main character(s) last), we can reduce the number of frames in animated image sequences. For instance, if we have a sequence that is 30 fps, we can delete every other frame (reducing it to 15 fps) and replace the image sequence for an object.

Music and sound optimization

When talking about music (or graphics), the word *optimal* is really a relative term. It's a matter of balancing the load of the asset (how large it is) against the quality of the asset. To ensure I get the best possible quality out of my sound while having my games meet the space restrictions, I follow this process:

1. **Work with sound last**: By doing sound at the end of your process, it not only lets you tailor your sound better for the graphics you created, but you have an idea of how much of that 100 MB limit you have left.

2. **Start high and end low**: Good, quality sound is highly overlooked (especially by some indie developers). Quality sound is something that can really give your game the feel you want: scary, uplifting, anticipation…all can be achieved with great sound. Bad sound can just be distracting. So, since the sound format for Buildbox is MP3, we should start with at least DVD-quality sound (128 Kb/s, 16-bit, 48 Khz). If the music and sound proves to be too much, we bring it down one setting at a time (128/16/44.1, then down to 96/16/44.1, then finally 64/16/44.1). Just don't go below 64 Kb/s. Anything lower will sound just…terrible. At that point, consider reducing the length and quantity of sound.

3. **Keep the music slightly lower than the sound effects**: Although it makes no difference on the size of your project, it's still a best practice. By keeping the music around 5-10 dB lower than your sound effects, your players will be able to hear everything going on, as well as the music.

Game template quick reference

We created the following chart to help you decide which game template to start with to create your games:

Game Template	Description	Template Screenshot
360 Shooter	The character can turn in any direction, and the screen may stay static or scroll.	
Around the World	Character walks on the surface of a shape (completely around, rather than just on top). For example, a planet that the character walks on to avoid obstacles.	
Avoidance	Character moves (generally progressively faster) through an obstacle course while avoiding the sides and all obstacles.	
Dogfight	Moves vertically while avoiding obstacles and shooting at enemies.	
Downward Bounce	Think of this like dribbling a basketball. Gravity is in effect, but touching the screen shoots the ball down toward the ground to have it bounce off the platform.	
Fall Buttons/Fall Switch	These are essentially the same game: guide a character falling down an obstacle course. Fall buttons use UI buttons, and fall switch operates by tapping anywhere on the screen.	

Flappy	Guide a character through a horizontally-scrolling screen while avoiding obstacles by *flapping* (tapping the screen or a button to give an upward boost to fight gravity).	
Gravity Portal	Run character along a platform to avoid obstacles. Switch gravity and fly up through top of screen, back through bottom, and run on the other side of the platform.	
Gravity Runner	Pretty much the same as gravity portal, but instead of going off screen, you can run along the ceiling or floor.	
Impossible	Intimidating name, right? This is essentially a platformer game wherein movement across the map is forced. Hop to avoid obstacles and enemies.	
ISO Jump/ISO Jump Slide	These are Isometric (2.5D) games. Built like a platformer, jump over obstacles, or (in jump slide) slide under them.	
Jet Pack	Think of this as a platformer fused with flappy. Run on the platform, or fly using flappy style flight to avoid obstacles.	

Jumping	Guide a jumping character up the map going from platform to platform and see how high you can go.	
Motorcross	Drive a vehicle over land, take jumps, and do tricks and flips.	
Platformer	Classic *Mario*-style game. Run across the ground, jump over obstacles, and onto platforms to avoid enemies.	
Racing	You could make a game like *Spyhunter* with this template. Guide your race car down a course while avoiding obstacles.	
Runner/ Shooting Runner	Runners are very similar to platformers. However, they generally move progressively faster, and usually don't have upper levels. Run through and jump over obstacles. Shooting runners usually add enemies, and the ability to shoot them.	
Side Shooter	Side shooters are very similar to dogfight games, but horizontal. Think *Gallaga*.	

Stage Clear	This is what you'd start with for a game like Pac Man or Jawbreaker. Consume all the coins to clear a world.	
Sticky Jump	Move a character through a map by jumping. When the character is on the ground, it stops. It only moves forward while in the air.	
Wall Jump	Very much the same as gravity reverse (but vertical). Guide your character and avoid obstacles by changing which wall attracts the character.	
Wall Reverse	Move the character to a goal object using flappy-style vertical movement while it bounces off the left and right walls.	
Zig Zag	Very similar to wall jump. Guide your character up a map while it moves left or right. Switch the lateral direction by tapping the screen.	

Platform restrictions

Use the following chart for reference on the restrictions for the various platforms:

Platform	Restrictions
iOS	• Must be < 100 MB • Can't use Made for Kids in iTunes Connect (yet)
Android/Amazon App	• Must be < 100 MB
Windows Store	• Only Vungle advertising
Steam	• No advertising

Troubleshooting games

Use the following chart to help you troubleshoot the most common issues with your game(s):

Issue	Possible solutions
Bullets destroy platforms	• Increase health of platforms to 99
Character can't walk across multiple platform objects without jumping	• Check the y-position of the platforms to make sure they are the same • Zoom in to walking surfaces to make sure they're level • Test the game using Debug Mode to make sure the collision shapes of the platforms match up
Portals don't work	• Increase the **Search Radius** so that both portals can recognize each other
Motorcross: the vehicle flips over whenever accelerating	• Increase the **Gravity** • Decrease the **Traction** • Decrease the **Time Warp**
Compiling in Eclipse: Version code error	• In Eclipse, open your project and find AndroidManifest.xml. Change the Version Code from 0 to 1

Characters pass through obstacles	• Check the **Destroy Type** in the obstacles' parameters • Check the **Collide** parameter to make sure it is `Collide`
Image sequences play too fast/slow	• Edit the **Speed** parameter in the Animation Editor.
Game is over the size limit for a platform	• Remove all unused assets using all the options in the Tools menu • Optimize the graphics (as outlined in this chapter) • Optimize the audio (as outlined in this chapter)

OMG... are we really done?!!

WOW! Congratulations are in order! It's been a long journey, but you've made it through this entire book. In this chapter, we've learned how to optimize our games and given you some quick reference charts to create games, understand the limitations of some of the platforms, and troubleshoot the most common issues with games created with Buildbox.

We sincerely thank you for your investment in this book and hope that this book has helped you navigate Buildbox. It is also our deep hope that it has shown you some aspects that have sparked your imagination on games you will create with Buildbox. Share your games with me! I'd love to see the games you create, and hear about how you've used this book. You can contact me via the Buildbox forums (`http://www.buildbox.com/forum`). My user name is `tyris_audronis`.

Thank you again, and get creating!

Index

D

damage point 159
Developer Console
    reference link 216
different rules
    setting up, for each world 140

E

End User License Agreement (EULA) 70
equipment prerequisites
    about 8
    development environment, complete
        specifications 9
    distribution channel memberships 10

F

First Person Shooter (FPS) 5
fiverr
    reference link 9
Flappy Bird game
    creating 270
frames
    keyframe 175
    tween 175
free sound effects
    reference link 192

G

Gallaga 273
game assets
    optimizing 214
game issues
    troubleshooting 287
Game Mind Map
    game over screen, creating 31, 32, 34, 36
    nodes 30
    using 29, 30
game over screen
    creating 31, 32, 34, 35
    game fonts, modifying 36, 37, 38, 39
    navigation button, setting up 39, 40
Game Over UIs
    about 34, 170
    menu, animating 174

Start UI (splash screen) 180
game template
    references 283
game types, in stock template
    360 Shooter 15
    Around the World 15
    avoidance 15
    default 14
    Dog Fight 15
    Downward Bounce 15
    Fall Buttons 15
    Fall Switch 15
    flappy 15
    Gravity Portal 15
    Gravity Runner 15
    impossible 15
    ISO Jump 15
    ISO Jump Slide 15
    Jetpack 15
    Jumping 15
    motocross 16
    platformer 16
    racing 16
    runner 16
    Shooting Runner 16
    Stage Clear 16
    Sticky Jump 16
    Wall Jump 16
    Wall Reverse 16
    Zig-Zag 16
games, based on platforms
    limitations 6
    platforms, for Buildbox games 6
GIMP
    reference link 8
Gliese 581D
    bump jump 144
    bumps 142
    conveyer chop 145
    Gliese secret level 146
    lava jump 142
    moosquatch 001 scene 143
    physics, setting up 141
    scene's characteristics 141
    Shaman Moosquatch 145, 146

www.ingramcontent.com/pod-product-compliance
Lightning Source LLC
Chambersburg PA
CBHW062108050326
40690CB00016B/3255